Striving Together Publications
4020 E. Lancaster Blvd.
Lancaster, CA 93535
800.201.7748

Cover design by Andrew Jones
Layout by Craig Parker and Beth Lee
Edited by Amanda Michael and Monica Bass
Special thanks to our proofreaders

ISBN 978-1-59894-169-2

Printed in the United States of America

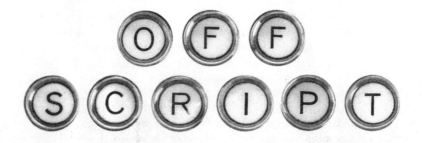

OFF SCRIPT

what to do

when God

rewrites your life

cary schmidt

DEDICATION

To Dana
You have amazed me in this trial!

Thank you for walking this difficult road by my side
with such unconditional love, unstoppable grace,
unmatched humor, unwavering faith
and unbelievable companionship!

You are angelic, and I love you more
than words could express!

CONTENTS

ACKNOWLEDGMENTS VII

FOREWORD IX

PREFACE XIII

INTRODUCTION XV

ONE—Love God, Trust God, Live for God 1

TWO—Be of Good Cheer 21

THREE—Be the Clay 39

FOUR—Cherish the Treasures of Darkness . . . 57

FIVE—Walk in the Spirit 81

SIX—Wait for Him, Hope in Him 101

SEVEN—Try Your Ways 121

EIGHT—Be Strong and Work 143

NINE—Love Your Own 163

TEN—Strive Together for the Faith 183

CONCLUSION 197

ACKNOWLEDGMENTS

A book requires a lot of work from an excellent team of people. It's a wonderful process and a joy to serve the Lord with such a great team.

First, I want to thank my family and my wife Dana for helping me find those quiet writing times. Dana, thank you for listening to ideas and for sharing your valuable insight as you read the first draft. And thanks for putting up with all the times I wanted to read out loud to you!

Second, I want to thank Pastor Paul Chappell for allowing me to serve in overseeing Striving Together Publications. It's a great joy and a dream come true to be a part of creating so many books and resources to encourage Christians in their spiritual growth.

Next, I wish to thank my secretary, Amanda Michael, and one of our lead writers and editors for Striving Together, Monica Bass. Thank you for pre-reading and re-reading the first and second drafts of these chapters as they were being written. Your professional insight and editorial input was invaluable!

Thank you to the select few who previewed this manuscript for press. Your insight and critique proved to be very valuable! Thank you for investing the time.

Thank you to Craig Parker and Beth Lee for their labor and detailed efforts in creating a beautiful layout. Thank you to Andrew Jones for your design of an engaging cover. Thank you to Sarah Michael and our ministry team of volunteer proofreaders who focused so excellently on helping us get the details correct.

Finally, thank you to the Lancaster Baptist Church family. Your love, encouragement, and prayers during our trial has contributed much to our family! We love you and and count it a joy to serve the Lord with you!

FOREWORD

EVERY PASTOR KNOWS THAT LIFE-CHANGING news is often just one phone call away. But we don't usually expect that call when it comes. I was sitting with a group of pastors in a restaurant in Australia when my phone rang. I glanced at the screen and was mildly surprised to see the name of Cary Schmidt, one of our associate pastors. Excusing myself from the table, I answered the phone.

After a cheerful greeting, as usual, Brother Schmidt explained the reason for his call. "Pastor, I recently had a CT scan that indicates cancer. We're still waiting on some more tests." And so began a season of suffering for the Schmidt family that none of us would have chosen or planned.

Cary Schmidt is like a son in the faith to me. I had the privilege of being his high school principal, and when our family moved to Lancaster in the summer before his senior year, Cary helped us load the Ryder truck and rode down with us. He then asked if he could stay for a couple of weeks to help. He assisted me in many hours of soulwinning and in church renovation, and he played the piano for those first few church services. Four years and a Bible college diploma later, Cary and his new bride Dana returned to Lancaster to serve on our staff. It has been a joy to watch him grow in the Lord and mature in ministry.

It would be impossible to detail the ways Brother Schmidt has helped me and our church family over the years. He serves in so many areas of ministry on a daily basis—youth, college and career, publications, radio, music, and more. He has worked diligently and tirelessly to teach our youth Bible truths in the context of a biblical ministry philosophy, and he has labored to make these truths available to other churches and Christians through Striving Together Publications.

Brother Schmidt is incredibly gifted, and he uses his spiritual gifts as he pours his life into others. Yet, in these past seven months, I've seen a growth in his life as only severe suffering can accelerate. G. Campbell Morgan once commented about another preacher, "He is a very good preacher, and when he has suffered, he will be a great preacher!" There is a work in our lives that only adversity can produce, and our entire church has been privileged to watch the Lord's work of grace in the Schmidt family through this trial of cancer.

There are times in all of our lives when God uses the pen of affliction to rewrite our life's story. But not all have responded to these unexpected chapters with the grace Brother Schmidt has. With an obvious anointing of grace, Cary has picked up his own pen and, tracing the new story God has been writing for his life, wrote for us on how to respond to trials. Few people I know would be able to write such a book from the midst of the trial, but I'm thankful he has.

This book will help you in your "off script" season. It is written by a skilled writer who is allowing God to control not only his pen, but his responses and emotions as well. And through these pages, he shares how you can do the same—how you can rest in the Lord through the trial, trusting Him all the way.

Brother Schmidt's testimony through this trial has left an indelible message in all of our hearts who have been able to share the trial with him. That message is the message of this book—trust God, rejoice in Him, and watch Him transform your trial. I know it will be a profound help and encouragement to you.

Paul Chappell
Lancaster, California
May 2011

PREFACE

THIS BOOK IS A DROP OF WATER IN AN OCEAN of encouragement from people of God who have suffered throughout the history of God's work in the lives of men.

My story is just one of millions who could share similar testimonies of God's grace in hardship. And my affliction has been rather light compared to hundreds of people I know personally. I make no claims at being a pro at trials. I'm no authority on pain and do not pretend that my trial is a very difficult one. I know many heroes who have suffered far greater adversity over many years.

I am nobody. And anything good on these pages is about God and His goodness. Recently, God has done many things in my life through a struggle with cancer, and these chapters are my meager attempt to share those truths and to shine some light on His goodness. Understand that these words flow from a sincere heart, trying to encourage, and desperate to learn more of these very truths myself.

Throughout this book I share stories from my journey—some funny and some sober. The stories I share are in no way complaints. They are merely given to provide transparent context for the truth of God and how it relates to the storms of life. Hopefully some of these accounts will make you laugh—laughter is good for your whole life!

The stories of others have encouraged me during this season. Perhaps my story will encourage you or someone you know.

Thank you for reading. Perhaps you know someone who is suffering hardship who might benefit from these truths. Pass it along if God leads.

May God bless you in your off script season of life.

INTRODUCTION

That the trial of your faith, being much more precious
than of gold that perisheth, though it be tried with fire,
might be found unto praise and honour and glory
at the appearing of Jesus Christ:—1 PETER 1:7

SNOWFLAKES FALL JUST OUTSIDE MY WINDOW— gently, silently, beautifully finding their rest upon gradually growing rows of white. Sun has set. Temperatures have dropped. A new year has dawned; the house is quiet. I am alone as I write these words. This is a Sunday night like I've never experienced. Normally for my life—the only script I've known—I would be in church.

Tonight happens to be "Vision Night"—the first Sunday night of the new year. My role, usually, is to be immersed with the team in the energy, the spirit, and the development of this exciting service—from planning, to media, to special music, to new year goals. But not this time. For the first time in twenty-one years, I am removed from this script. It moves on without me. It's surreal.

This night is beautiful but cold. It's snowing in the desert. Outside my window is a wonderland of snow on an icy evening. A paradox. A conflict. The child in me wants to don wintery clothing and rush into the billowing flakes with innocent abandon. The more rational adult in me feels the cold, the wet, the dark—the starkness of the elements, the dangers of the night, the unknowns of the storm. Part of me wants to laugh and play in the beauty of the snow, but part of me wants to stay safe and close to a warm fire and forget about the bitter cold just outside.

And such is my life. Beautiful, but cold at the moment. Storming outside, but warm inside. Outside it is stark, cloudy, dangerous, and risky—leading to unknown outcomes. Just outside of my reach—beyond anything I can control—life has become messy and icy. It has become wintery gray. But that's not the whole picture. There's a certain beauty here as well. There's something inviting, something of sovereignty, grace, strength, and purpose etched in patterned snowflakes that fall on my soul.

The sky is falling, but beautifully so. There's a warmth, a glow, an embrace that shelters me from the raging storm that God has ordained. And sheltered from the storm, there are beautiful moments, incredible relationships, blessed details that infuse my life from every direction. I couldn't ask for a greater blizzard of blessings on a cold winter night.

Hence, the paradox—winter and snow. Winter: cold, icy, and treacherous at times. Snow: light, beautiful, and even delightful.

The storm is cancer. The diagnosis and the present treatments and side-effects have descended upon my life, family, and ministry like an unexpected winter storm—in many ways sequestering me and holding me hostage from the life I have known for a long time. Unpredictable has become the norm.

In the storm, I wrestle with things beyond my control. I wrestle with feeling removed from the "doing" of ministry. I wrestle with feeling useless to those around me. I wrestle with the remaining months of difficult treatments ahead. I wrestle with knowing there are no guarantees of outcomes— no certainty of healing, no promise of remission, no assurance that cancer will never return. I wrestle with the sadness of being a burden to others. I wrestle with not being able to participate with my church family in normal body life. I wrestle with having no energy and not being able to function normally during treatment weeks. I wrestle with concern for my wife Dana and my children. I wrestle with even dreaming about the future—will I be here for it? I wrestle with this wintery experience of life.

I wrestle, not with a bad attitude or wrong spirit, but with the unfamiliar nature of these experiences. I can't say that I like them. I accept them, but each of them, in their own way, wraps their ghoulish arms around my spirit attempting to wrench my heart away from faith and hope. They may attempt, but by God's grace, they will not succeed.

Inside, safe from the storm, near the warmth of the fire, I do not wrestle. I rest. In God's presence, with the warmth of His grace and the strength of His embrace, there is no wrestling. The uncertainty remains. The elements remain. Circumstances beyond my control continue. The questions remain unanswered. The trial remains unabated. The future remains uncertain and gray. But near the heart of God, everything is different.

It is His sovereignty that makes the difference.

The storm is in His hand. The flakes fall from His fingers. The cold comes from His control. The struggle streams from His sovereign plan. And He is good.

Off Script

We all have a script for our lives. It resides in our minds and hearts—perhaps a good bit in our imaginations. And we're generous to ourselves there. Things are good in our script. Stuff works out. Events unfold in our favor. Circumstances are easily manipulated in our minds. In a human sense, it may be fantasy. In a more biblical sense, it may be hope and vision. Either way, in our hearts, we usually don't daydream about the trials we will one day face. No one gets sick, people don't die, nothing bad happens in our mental screenplays. Our scripts are predictable and positive, and sanitized of trouble.

And, in God's good grace, He often allows much of what we envision to actually happen. A lot of what you planned last week, last month, or last summer probably came to pass. The majority of your script probably unfolded just as you wrote it.

But if we're honest with our hearts, we know that a trouble-free script is not realistic. Every now and then, God takes our lives off script. He reaches into our circumstances with events we never imagined and factors we would never choose. He leads us into intersections where the path of our expectations collides with the path of His choosing—places where He doesn't follow our predetermined dreams.

These unexpected adventures are often alarming, painful, uncomfortable, and scary. Sometimes we think of them as detours. We immediately start strategizing how we can get back onto our own script. At other times, the irreversible events that unfold make returning to our script entirely impossible. But these off script journeys are anything but detours, for they are intricately a part of His script—His heart and purpose for our lives.

Recently, God took my life suddenly off script. The coming chapters will describe how He has done so in more detail. I would have never expected to be writing these words from this place. Frankly, it's bizarre. There's a part of my human logic that still has a hard time wrapping my brain around the word "cancer" and all of its implications—both short term and long term. My script would have never unfolded as the last few months have, and as the future seems to be. And yet, like a winter storm, there are elements of both struggle and strength, burden and blessing, trouble and triumph in this place of uncertainty.

When God takes our lives off script (and He does with all of us eventually) we enter a most unusual paradox. Hardship and storms either flatten us or fortify us. They become catalysts that thrust us in one of two directions—closer to God and forward in growth in His grace, or further from God in doubt and despair. Off script seasons teach us much, reveal in us even more, and call us to deeper and different living. These are not trivial times. They are pivotal. They are defining moments, and their implications are huge!

These pages flow from the midst of an off script life. The raw experience of sickness and uncertainty is ever present and very real. I write with no certainty of the outcome and no knowledge of where this journey is leading—what kind of struggle, medical procedures, test results, or physical developments lie ahead. This is the middle—or perhaps, the very beginning—of the trial. It's far from over.

And it's from this position that I hope these words will be an encouragement to your life. If your world has gone awry, if your life is off script, perhaps together we can discover God's heart, God's joy, and God's truth in the fog of an uncertain reality. If your life hasn't gone off script, perhaps these chapters will prepare you for the moment that it does. Either way, I'm choosing intentionally to write from within the trial. Why?

First, because so many of God's servants did so with raw and unvarnished reality. Much of God's Word speaks to us from the middle of His children's trials. We will see some of these passages up close.

Second, because I have no guarantee that I will be able to write "after the trial"—whenever and if ever that may be.

Third, because right now the trial is very fresh and real. The presence of God is more so! The place where God has led me in recent months is abundant with both hurt and hope, struggle and strength, and I'd like to share what He is teaching me.

Finally, because speaking from the midst of my light affliction, I can be a bit bolder to speak to you in the midst of yours, and challenge you in ways that God is challenging me.

PROVIDENTIAL PAUSE

Outside, the snow is no longer falling. The night is quiet and still. The landscape is draped in white, and the night glows with a radiance of peace and solitude. The storm that was, now holds the night in a still, ghostly blanket. It's as if the sky is holding its breath, awaiting instructions. It's as if the world is wondering "what next?"

Will the night last forever? Will the icy hold remain unchanged through the morning? Or will the warm rays of the morning sun instruct the night freeze to break its chains? How long will this icy pause last? How long before spring blossoms with new life and energy?

How long? God knows how long—and that is enough. He has ordained the winter. He has chosen the cold. He has called the storm. It's really up to Him. As long as He desires. As long as He requires. As long as it takes Him to accomplish His purposes. Winter is in His hands, and thankfully I am too.

So I accept this pause—this life that has gone wildly off script. Having no idea what God is really doing, where I am, or where I'm headed, I admire the artistry of God's paradoxical power—the beauty of His grace and majesty, unveiled amidst the coldness of a wintery trial.

Just outside my window are bare-limbed trees covered in layers of white flakes. At the tips of every limb is a tiny bulb—a blossom waiting to open. But those blossoms are held hostage. The winter has enfolded them and refuses their potential. But they are there. Waiting. Patient. And they give evidence of new life and growth in the days ahead. About the time I'm done writing this book, those bulbs will be beautifully blossoming in the sun-filled arms of spring.

Even so, I belong to a God who has filled my life with bountiful, abundant, innumerable blessings that are now held like expectant blossoms in a still white blanket of cold interruption. Suspended. Halted. Awaiting instructions. I look forward to spring, but for now life is blessedly halted. Graciously interrupted by Divine interlude. Suspended by nothing less than the hand of God. Held in a providential pause that is dark and cold, but also in a sovereign hand that is good and gracious.

And so I resolve to rest. I choose to trust. I determine to walk this wintery path, hoping for spring but marveling in the midnight.

This is not the script I imagined. This is not the script I was writing. This is not the script I hoped for. But this is the script my Father has ordained for my life.

Let's examine and embrace ten decisions that will transform our lives in times of trial. Let's discover what to do when God rewrites the script of your life!

ONE

LOVE GOD, TRUST GOD, LIVE FOR GOD

When thou passest through the waters, I will be with thee; and through the rivers, they shall not overflow thee:—ISAIAH 43:2

DANA'S VOICE WAS URGENT—"CARY, IT'S THE doctor." I looked at the clock—9 PM. Gulp.

What doctor calls at 9 PM to tell you that you're healthy? Immediately, my heart was in my throat, and I could tell by the look on Dana's face, hers was too. I grabbed the phone, rushed up the stairs, closed the bedroom door and said, "Hello...."

In his thick Russian accent, the doctor hurriedly explained that my CT scan earlier that day revealed "spots in your lungs... correction... spots in between your lungs and across your chest. We are referring you to oncology/ hematology for biopsy. Okay? Okay... bye...."

1

"Whoa! Hold on a minute!" I could tell he didn't want any questions. "What do you think this is?" I pushed back a surge of adrenaline.

"It's really too early to tell, and I don't want to speculate because I'm just going from what the technician told me. I haven't seen the results. You should schedule an appointment with your regular doctor. Okay? Okay... bye."

That was it. A Russian in a hurry—spots, oncology, biopsy—this is the stuff of cancer. Phone in one hand, my other hand rubbing my chest, I looked at Dana and we were numb. Circumstances were rapidly unfolding to reveal to us a complete and unexpected turn in the script of our lives.

REWIND...

The story begins in the winter of 2009. Usually, at least twice a year, I'm good for a strong case of bronchitis. This winter was no different, except for the fact that the antibiotics that normally quickly wipe it out, only masked the symptoms. The cough and chest congestion went away, but something was different—I even mentioned it to the doctor. For the following eighteen months I was always two or three days away from another chest cough, heaviness, and tightness of breath. When I rested, the symptoms subsided. When I pushed myself, they returned immediately. This was different than my normal semi-annual bronchial bouts.

So I remained functional by managing the symptoms with rest and over-the-counter medications. I basically chalked it up as age—after all, everybody told me that things would start to change after my fortieth birthday. Every afternoon by about three-o-clock I could feel my chest getting heavy and fatigue setting in. Coffee became a new best friend to provide that afternoon zap of energy. But in my heart I was uneasy with these changes.

With the dawn of a new year, 2010, I began to notice something else—swollen lymph nodes. I could feel two of them under my arm, and then a month or so later, another one on my collarbone. I'm optimistic, and healthy, so I thought nothing of them. They even changed size from time to time, and went away. But not for good. They kept coming back. It was usually at night, sitting in bed with Dana, that I would feel them. "I think I need to have these looked at...." She concurred, but neither one of us was in a hurry.

Spring flew by with all of its ministry and family activity. We enjoyed a wonderful summer and our church's annual Spiritual Leadership Conference, followed by family vacation. By July the lymph nodes and unusual fatigue were pretty much sticking around, and another symptom showed up—itching. Some surface itching and sores began on my hands, elbows, knees and ankles, and that was followed by deep, below-the-surface itching in my hands and feet. Never connecting these symptoms, I assumed I was developing an allergy to something. Creams and ointments were useless, changing soaps did nothing, and I mentioned to Dana that I wanted to see an allergist after vacation. One night in particular I looked up the itching online. All the medical sites indicated that I was either allergic to something, diabetic, or had lymphoma.

Well, I know I don't have lymphoma! I thought. I didn't even mention this possibility to Dana. I didn't want to worry her. Frankly, I didn't give it a second thought because I had no other symptoms of lymphoma. I really believed I was just allergic—probably to Dana's cooking.

By late August, vacation had passed, and I was sitting in an allergist appointment waiting to hear that my wife needed to change one of her recipes. You know, it's one of those routines where they prick your arm in 42 places to see which areas start to itch. Sitting there itching bad enough to start biting my arm, it turned out that I am allergic to everything in the desert where I live—trees, tumbleweeds, dust—and believe it or not, peaches.

"Well, some things are worth itching for—and peaches are one of them!" I told my wife. But the real moment of truth in the appointment was when the doctor looked at the sores on my hands and elbows and said, "That's not an allergy."

That bothered me. I didn't show it. But I had read the possibilities, and the other options weren't good.

We scheduled a physical for September. I still never connected the dots, but in retrospect it's clear. Knowing what I now know about lymphoma, I should have asked for a CT scan early in 2010. Hindsight is always 20/20, right? The physical was uneventful, except for the fact that the Russian doctor referred me for a CT scan. "It could be a lot of things, don't worry," he said, "but we should have CT scan to know for sure."

Eleven days later, I had the scan in the afternoon, and at 9 PM received that rushed and alarming phone call. Realizing now that something was really wrong, Dana and I prayed together, said nothing to the kids, and immediately scheduled an appointment with my regular physician, who is also a friend of ours, for Wednesday evening.

THE STORY BEHIND THE STORY

About twelve years ago, I was shaking hands in the lobby of our church when a young, visiting couple approached me— Joseph and Juliet. I introduced myself, shook their hands, and discovered that they had recently come from Kenya, and Joseph was pursuing a medical degree at UCLA. After a few moments of small talk, I asked them if they had heard the end of Pastor Chappell's message about salvation. "Do you know for sure that you are going to Heaven?"

Joseph was a bit surprised by the question, and in his thick Kenyan accent, asked, "Can you know that?"

I smiled, "Well, according to the Bible, yes you can. Would you like to?"

They both smiled and he replied, "If you can know, then yes!"

I immediately found a faithful member of our church, asked him to share the Gospel with Joseph and Juliet, and about thirty minutes later, I stepped into the back of the auditorium just in time to see them bow their heads to accept Jesus Christ as their Saviour. It was a precious moment that I will never forget.

Little did I know that some years later, Joseph would become my doctor, and he would give me the most disturbing news I had ever received.

Disturbing News

Two days after that 9 PM phone call, we were sitting in Joseph's office watching him review the CT images and read the report. As he studied the tests, I remembered our first meeting in the church lobby so many years prior. I was still expecting him to tell me this was something simple— something easily fixed. But no such news. He turned the screen, and read the words, "8.6 centimeter mediastinal mass" in addition to other smaller masses across both sides of my chest and under my right arm.

My mind raced, not with panic, but with urgency to gather every spiritual truth and promise of God—to draw on a lifetime of hearing Bible teaching. My spirit began reaching out to the Lord for strength and grace for what we were about to hear.

"Doctor, what's a best-case/worst-case scenario? What are we looking at here?" I asked.

With a careful pause he said, "Worst case, you are looking at non-Hodgkin's lymphoma, which is a cancer, and is about 30 percent survivable. Best case, I say, would be Hodgkin's lymphoma, a cancer which is about 95 percent survivable."

Cancer? Did I hear him right? He wasn't leaving room for a simpler option. I was taken back. What about allergies, infections? What about Dana's cooking? Surely I can change laundry detergents and this will go away. "So, you *really believe* this is cancer?"

I will never forget his response, "I am 90 percent sure that you have lymphoma."

Slowly, I sat back in my chair, looked at Dana, and we were speechless.

A few moments later we stepped into the hall, I put my arm around my wife, and she buried her head in my chest, weeping. It was a long walk to the car, and I did my best to comfort her, tell her not to worry, and explain that this will all be okay. Though I really had no idea.

We drove to a local soccer park and walked. We held each other, we talked about the journey ahead, we prayed, we wept, and we began to call family and friends. A million thoughts were racing through our minds. But someone met us there. A Friend came and began speaking peace, resolve, and calm into this off script experience. The Holy Spirit of God, as real and tangible as another human being, met us in that unsettled moment and began to shape our response with His peace and comfort.

"Dana, I don't know what's ahead, but I know a few things." We were walking, arm in arm, and we paused to lean against a chain-link fence. "I know we are in the Lord's hands. I know He has a good plan in this. I know we will honor Him. And whatever His will is in my life, I just want to run my race and finish my course. Whatever He plans, we will serve Him and joyfully honor Him."

Through tears of resolve she agreed. I continued, "We will do everything the doctors say, and if God heals me, then I will live for Him and serve Him; but if God has other plans," I fumbled for words and thoughts—this was tough to say, "I'm not going to live in denial or lead our family and friends in denial. If God wants to take me home early, I want to die joyfully for Him and show others that trials and death are not despairing events for a Christian. Either way, I want to do this for the Lord—I belong to Him and when I gave Him my life so long ago, I meant it."

We prayed together, and covenanted with God and with each other to do this His way—by His grace—wherever this script was headed. Terrified—a little. Trusting—most definitely. Tormented—absolutely not. Life was suddenly way *off script*, but not out of God's hands. And long ago I determined I would rather be in God's hands than on my own script.

Love God, Trust God, Live for God

An hour later we waited at home for our three children to return from church. We had debated when and how to tell them. Should we wait for the biopsy? Could we hide the concern that long? The Lord seemed to say, "Do it tonight—the sooner the whole family is praying, the better."

I think this was the hardest moment of my entire life—up to the point of this writing. How do I tell my kids that Dad has cancer? I simply begged God for wisdom and strength—wisdom to say the right things, strength to say them with joy and hope, no matter the outcome.

My kids are good at reading us, so the minute they walked in the door, Lance said, "What's wrong?" Something in our faces gave it away—maybe the tear streaks and swollen eyes were a good clue. Larry and Haylee were just behind him and they asked the same question. I smiled and said, "Don't worry about it, we just need to have a family talk."

A few moments later, we gathered in the family room, I held Dana's hand, and the kids waited with alarmed expressions. Slowly I explained to the kids that the Lord was leading us into a trial. I shared the story you have just read, and carefully studied their responses. First, we wept. We all sort of collapsed in each others arms and just let some emotions flow. Then I explained how we would face this as a family.

"First, guys, I want you to know, this is probably Hodgkin's lymphoma which is very curable." I was wrong about the probability, and Dana knew it. I had misunderstood the doctor. Hodgkin's is less common than non-Hodgkin's.

"Second, I want you guys to know, a trial is like a precious treasure that God places in our hands and loans to us. It's a trust—a sacred trust. It's an opportunity to show His grace and goodness to others, and to be used by God in a very special way. God doesn't give trials to someone unless He has a special plan to use it. And this means He wants to use us—so I want us to respond the right way and honor the Lord through this.

"Third, I'm not going to lie. There's a chance that this could take my life. It probably won't, but it could. If it does, that's probably a long time from now, and we don't need to worry about it yet. We can prepare for it, but we don't need to think a lot about it.

"Finally, here's what we're going to do—as a family. Three things: we are going to *love God*, we are going to *trust God*, and we are going to *live for God*—no matter what, for the rest of our lives." I repeated myself, two more times, "*Love God, trust God, live for God, no matter what, for the rest of our lives.*"

"Guys, to me, there's something much worse than dying. And that would be for anyone in this family to become bitter at God or to grow up not loving and living for God because of this trial. I want us to promise each other, right here, right now, that we will do these three things for the rest of our lives."

Then, one by one, I looked deeply into the eyes of my children. I called them by name. I asked them each for a promise. "No matter what happens, even if I die, do you promise me you will love God, trust God, and live for God as long as you live?" One by one they promised. Then in agreement we bowed our heads, and one at time, we prayed, each promising God our love, trust, and lives, and asking Him to help us not become bitter. It was special—a moment I thank God for and one we will never forget.

This is how the story began.

I could barely wrap my brain around it—cancer. I'm forty-one, healthy, and busy! I don't do cancer—I help encourage people with cancer. I don't have time for cancer, I'm serving God in ministry—a busy, dynamic, growing ministry. I'm raising my family for the Lord. Cancer was nowhere in my script.

And yet, this is no dream. As surreal as it is, it is really happening.

CHOOSING TO RESPOND

Has your life gone "off script" by God's design? Have you found yourself suddenly taking a journey, experiencing circumstances, and bearing burdens you would have never chosen? Off script—those times when life becomes completely unpredictable and God seemingly removes all normalcy from our routines. These moments are among the most critical of our lives. They are pivotal, life-changing, heart-wrenching, direction-setting times. They are life defining.

If you have entered a scene of life you didn't expect, you have stepped into a "God moment." But you've also stepped into a very precarious and vulnerable time. What you do next and how you respond could make or break the rest of your life. Many people let off script seasons take their lives far off course with anger, sorrow, despair, and bitterness. Off script times can lead to total meltdown and regret.

We cannot choose our trials, but we can always choose our responses. And in reality, this book is about response. This is

not a book that will help you get back on script. That may
be impossible. You may never get back on your script. I may
not either. I agree with you, that's hard to process. When we
enter off script times, our first thought is, "God, when will
you take this away so I can get back on script?" But in reality,
that may not happen. (Don't despair at that thought; just
keep reading.)

Four months ago, I had a pretty reliable script in the
works. Life was good and predictable. Ministry was fruitful,
family was healthy, my schedule was filled with incredible
ministry opportunities, and I was enjoying the script God
had allowed for my life. As of right now, that script doesn't
even exist anymore. I have no clue what God has in mind or
where this is going. Maybe you don't either.

So, I write to "us"—myself and you—those of us in the
off script experience of things we never thought would
happen to "us." What we do during this time is huge. Again,
we cannot control the script, but we can control how we
respond. And in these pages, I want to call you to the right
response—to do the right thing when God suddenly rewrites
your life.

Off script times, in God's will, are an adventure. They are
a trust. They are God times. God Himself has ordained the
events of our lives according to His eternal purpose, and He
has chosen you to journey with Him in a more intimate way,
to experience a richness of closeness with Him, to encounter

His grace and presence in a way never before experienced, and to walk with Him through difficulty that you might bring more glory to His name. He has chosen you to partner with Him for eternal good. He reaches out a hand to you, invites you off the pages of your script, and says, "Come with Me. I will be with you!"

I WILL BE WITH THEE

God promised to be with those who would remain faithful to Him in hardship. He said in Isaiah 43:2:

> *When thou passest through the waters, I will be with thee; and through the rivers, they shall not overflow thee: when thou walkest through the fire, thou shalt not be burned; neither shall the flame kindle upon thee.*

Not *if* you pass through waters, rivers, fire... but *when*. Expect it. Understand that passing through these things is a part of life—it will happen to you. "But, when you do, if you are mine, I will be with thee. You won't be overwhelmed. You won't be burned. You won't be destroyed. I'm going to sustain you, protect you, and be with you." Wow! What a great God.

Do you trust Him? Do you really believe that God is good, God is sovereign, God is loving, and that His plan for your life is better than your own? Can you fathom that He loves you more than you could ever imagine?

Has it occurred to you that what you face right now was always in the script—His script?

Can we accept the fact that in many ways our scripts are just our best guess? They are often just mere fantasy. But His script is eternal. It is real. It is good—ultimately good. And there is no better, no more purposeful, no more essential life than the one lived on God's script!

Before You Were Born...

I love how God called Jeremiah to serve Him. In Jeremiah 1:4–5, after a brief explanation of his background, Jeremiah, a young man, wrote these words:

> *Then the word of the LORD came unto me, saying,*
> *Before I formed thee in the belly I knew thee; and before*
> *thou camest forth out of the womb I sanctified thee, and*
> *I ordained thee a prophet unto the nations.*

God's Word is basically saying, "Jeremiah, God's script was written for your life before you came out of the womb. Before He formed you He knew you—He understood your personality, your abilities, your gifts. He custom designed you. And then He ordained you. He determined to call you into the ministry as His prophet."

Frankly, this was way off Jeremiah's script. He refutes the call in verse 6—"God, you have the wrong guy! I'm a child. I couldn't possibly speak for you!" Off script. Not what Jeremiah had planned.

We'll see later, these events took Jeremiah completely away from his life plan for the rest of his life. It was never the same. He never returned to his script. In fact, God's call was a heavy one—it was a call to suffer, to be rejected, to be tormented at times, and to face more trials than this book could describe! But God promised to be with him, to protect him, and to use him. God promised to enable him to walk through it all.

This was an all-out invitation from the God of the universe to join Him on a life adventure of eternal purpose and massive proportions. And at some point in the vicinity of chapter 1, Jeremiah was all in. He surrendered. He let go of his script and embraced God's—regardless of what it involved or where it led. Jeremiah trusted God's script more than his own.

How about you? How about me? Can we pull a "Jeremiah" here? Can you see God's hand extended in your trial? Can you hear Him inviting you away from your security, your safe zone? Can you hear Him say, "Come with me. There will be some waters to pass through, some rivers to cross, and some fire to withstand, but I promise to be with you. I promise you will not be overwhelmed. I will get you through this"?

Can you hear Him say to you, like to Jeremiah, "This was always in the script. Before I formed you, I knew you. Before you were born, I ordained this moment. Come with me and let me show you all that I have planned for your life"?

Jeremiah was one of the greatest servants of God known in human history. His message would have been the one that Daniel and others heard before going into captivity—a message of how to stay faithful to God in Babylon. His message was pivotal to preserving a generation of people— God's people, and ultimately bringing them back into their homeland.

Jeremiah made the right choice. He abandoned his script and embraced God's. How about you and me?

What do you do when God rewrites your life?

Decision one:
LOVE GOD, TRUST GOD, LIVE FOR GOD

Resolve with God to love Him, trust Him, and live for Him, no matter what, for the rest of your life.

I challenge you to make the same commitment that our family made. Make the same choice that Jeremiah made.

There are a million unanswered questions. There are a thousand circumstances we cannot control. The road ahead is foggy and unclear. We could respond with panic, fear, anxiety, murmuring, and despair; but what good would that do—really? We could freak out. We could mope. We could miss all of the delight and blessings of taking this journey with our loving Father.

And so, with all the unknowns that lie ahead for you, I invite you to make this decision. Commit to it. Determine your course of action.

"God, I will love you, trust you, and live for you, no matter what, for the rest of my life!"

Say it out loud. Mean it. Engrave it into your heart and your thoughts, never to be reconsidered:

"God, I am Yours, You are mine—we make this journey together, and I choose Your script. I surrender mine. You are God. I know You are good. You will be with me. Let's do this...."

I have no clue where my journey is heading. I've read of every possible outcome of my illness. Every one of them—from quick cure, to long struggle, to eventual death—is a very real possibility. For all I know, this could be the last book I ever write. All I know for certain is this—God is writing the script, and He is good.

For the rest of my life I want to love God, live for God, and trust God, no matter what.

I hope you do too.

IN CHRIST ALONE

In Christ alone my hope is found,
He is my Light, my Strength, my Song;
This Cornerstone, this solid Ground,
Firm through the fiercest drought and storm.
What heights of love, what depths of peace,
When fears are stilled, when strivings cease!
My Comforter, my All in All,
Here in the love of Christ I stand.

In Christ alone who took on flesh,
Fulness of God in helpless babe!
This gift of love and righteousness,
Scorned by the ones he came to save.
Till on that cross as Jesus died,
The wrath of God was satisfied—
For every sin on Him was laid;
Here in the death of Christ I live.

There in the ground His body lay,
Light of the world by darkness slain.
Then bursting forth in glorious day,
Up from the grave He rose again!
And as He stands in victory,
Sin's curse has lost its grip on me.
For I am His and He is mine—
Bought with the precious blood of Christ.

No guilt in life, no fear in death,
This is the power of Christ in me;

From life's first cry to final breath,
Jesus commands my destiny.
No power of hell, no scheme of man,
Can ever pluck me from His hand;
Till He returns or calls me home,
Here in the power of Christ I'll stand.

—STUART TOWNEND AND KEITH GETTY

TWO
BE OF GOOD CHEER

*But straightway Jesus spake unto them, saying, Be of
good cheer; it is I; be not afraid.*—Matthew 14:27

ONE THING I FOUND OUT AFTER THAT
Wednesday night appointment—the cancer script moves
really fast, especially when you have a wife determined to
keep you alive! The next day, Dana was immediately on the
phone with various medical departments following up on
necessary appointments to move toward an official diagnosis
and staging tests.

Step one was to get a biopsy of the lymph nodes to find
out what kind of cancer this was—we weren't sure if this
biopsy would involve surgery or not. Step two involved a
long list of tests to determine the staging or extent of the
cancer—how much of my body was involved.

Monday morning, October 4, was our first appointment with the surgeon. Pastor and Mrs. Chappell graciously drove us to the appointment and waited with us. A few nervous moments later, I was in the room with the surgeon who was preparing for what's called a "core-needle biopsy." The process was quick, relatively painless, and successful. He took two samples from the swollen nodes under my arm, didn't want to answer any questions, and hurriedly told me he would call me between Wednesday and Friday with the results.

The week really drags by when you're waiting for the phone call that basically tells you whether you can expect to live or die. Wednesday—no call. Thursday—no call. Friday—no call. Knowing that my health care system closes up shop around 5 PM, I waited until 4 PM. I called the surgeon's office only to be told by the nurse that he would probably call me Monday. That wasn't good enough.

FINALLY, A DIAGNOSIS...

Then I remembered Dr. Peram. She is one of the sweetest Christians I have ever met, a dear member of our church family, and just the week before she had given me her cell phone number and told me to call her if I needed anything. Because she had seen me prior, she had access to my medical records.

As the clock ticked 4:45, I decided to call Dr. Peram. I will never forget that phone call. In the middle of a meeting, staff members sitting in my office, I was making the most important phone call of my life. You see, by now I had done enough reading to discover that Hodgkin's is less common than non-Hodgkin's. And while both are beatable, Hodgkin's is far more so—at least statistically. This phone call, in my mind, sort of boiled down to either a "prepare to die, or prepare to live" sort of thing.

Dr. Peram picked up the call, was fortunately between patients, and happily looked up my biopsy results. Her gracious voice spoke with such compassion, "Brother Schmidt, you have classical Hodgkin's lymphoma." She paused. I threw my arms in the air, like my team had just won a championship game! I was celebrating—I probably get to live! This was great news.

"Brother Schmidt, I'm so sorry to be the one to tell you this…." She was trying to comfort me.

"No, no—Dr. Peram, it's okay! I already knew I had lymphoma. I'm just relieved to find out this is Hodgkin's. Thank you for your help!"

We finished our phone call and I continued my celebration. I looked at the people in my office, "I probably get to live!" Awkward moment. They didn't know whether to smile or not. I called Dana, "It's Hodgkin's!" She sighed with relief. I wrapped up my meeting and began updating family and friends.

While there are no guarantees by this diagnosis, it appeared that God's script was leading through a season of suffering that would likely (statistically) end in healing and longer life. And while I was and still am resolved to die in God's time and God's way—I can't lie—I was happy to discover that cure was a genuine possibility. I am in no hurry to die.

TESTS, STAGING, AND BEYOND

Thanks to my wifely, medical assistant, two days later, October 11 we had our first appointment with oncology/hematology—that's a cancer/blood doctor. Once again, Pastor Chappell met us at the doctor's office—what a comfort and help during a tough time. My oncologist began to explain the process. October would become a whirlwind of tests to determine the staging of this disease and to determine the condition of my body in preparation for chemotherapy and possibly radiation.

Toward the end of the appointment I asked the kind Nigerian doctor if he had a religion. He sheepishly admitted that he was a non-practicing Muslim. I shared some of the Gospel with him and promised to bring him a copy of *Done*—a book I had written about salvation. He agreed to read it.

I thanked him for helping me stay alive. And the appointment came to an end. Immediately I began to see that God had a much larger purpose in this than I could comprehend. Perhaps one of those purposes was helping this doctor come to Christ.

The next day, Dana was back on the phone scheduling more tests. The first was a MUGA scan—a test to clear my heart for chemo. The kind of chemo used to treat Hodgkin's poses certain risks and potential damage to the heart. So before they damage it, they want to make sure the heart is in good condition. What a blessing.

The next week, God allowed me to keep one more preaching trip—a youth conference in the Washington D.C. area. It was a welcome respite from the storm. My daughter Haylee went with me and we enjoyed four wonderful days together with friends, relatives, and the beautiful autumn sites of Washington, DC and the Maryland countryside. I tried to forget what was waiting for me back home—namely the dreaded bone marrow biopsy!

October 25 brought a PET scan and an MRI. The PET scan is the most important cancer test—it literally showed every area of my body that involved cancer and the degree or size of involvement—the results of this test would be critical to the staging and hopeful cure. The MRI was simply to verify that some previous lower back pain was not related to the cancer.

The next day was the Pulmonary Function Test—another name for the "we're gonna put you in a box and make you breath like an ape on steroids" test. This was one of the most hilarious experiences of my life, and I'm really glad no one has it on video! Until that test, I thought Lamaze class was the strangest breathing experience I'd ever had.

Amidst all of this, it would be impossible to recount all the support, prayers, and expressions of love that we received—literally from all over the world. Family, friends, pastors, and hundreds of Christians we have never even met began to flood our inboxes with love and encouragement. Honestly, it was overwhelming. I had so many people telling me they were praying for me I started to feel like a prayer hog! It was humbling to say the least.

CINNAMON ROLLS AND BONE MARROW

Wednesday, October 27, 2010 began with the cinnamon roll ministry. Savory, warm, gooey, and covered with icing—Heaven on earth. Sweetness epitomized. Field day for the taste buds. Respite from reality. Ah—God is good to have created such things.

We were running late for the doctor's appointment and the final test—the bone marrow biopsy. I must confess—I was dragging a bit on purpose that morning. I wasn't in too much of a hurry for someone to swipe a chunk of my bone marrow. Being the great caregiver that she is, Dana was pushing a little, trying to speed me up.

After we dropped the kids off at school, I had decided to stop by the donut shop, late or not. It was a coping mechanism. Something like a "last meal" before torture. As I pulled into the donut shop, Dana protested, "We're late... we don't have time."

"I'm sorry, this isn't up for negotiation," I smiled, "in a few minutes someone is going to be drilling into my hip. I need a cinnamon roll." That was all she needed to hear. It was a sweet, welcome pause before the pain.

Moments later, cinnamon roll moment past, I was in the doctor's office for a bone marrow biopsy. (Wait, rewind—let's go back to the icing part!) My first thought was—Dana can take this test for me—after all she's from my rib and the Bible says she's "bone of my bone," right!? (In all seriousness, she probably would have if she could—she's a great lady with a tender heart. I could never ask for a better companion through all this!)

The routine went like this—lay down on your stomach while we drill into your hip for a while, and we'll let you know when we're done. It was a slightly embarrassing procedure and a bit painful.

The doctor said, "You're going to experience some pressure...." Code language for prepare for pain! In the middle of it all, there's this dramatic pause. The doctor has stopped wrenching my torso, the nurses have stopped talking, everyone's waiting—so I said, "I'd like to take this moment to invite you all to visit my church…." It was a serious but comical moment for sure. I found out later the quiet moment was one where they were all looking at the drill/needle—it was bent!

As the test was completed, the doctor commented that he never had a patient with such hard bones—he had never had a bent needle. I said, "I guess I should have warned you about my steel infrastructure." That was the moment the doctor started calling me Superman. And through this all, I'm thankful God has given me a bit of a warped sense of humor. It sure helps in processing the otherwise stressful circumstances. Plus, I was pretty happy about that bent needle for some reason.

The bone marrow biopsy was, by far, the most serious test of all. If the lymphoma was in the bone marrow, that's as serious as it gets—stage four automatically. At that point the disease is systemic—throughout the whole body—still treatable, but a much more serious situation. We would have to wait ten more days for the results.

In all of these events, God certainly had sent me and my family into a storm. Fortunately, He meets us in our storms and speaks to us through His Word…

BE OF GOOD CHEER

In Matthew 14, Jesus' disciples are in a sinking boat in the middle of a deadly storm. They are sinking and scrambling to avoid destruction. They are anxious and overwhelmed—focused on survival. Their world is chaos, confusion, and desperation. And in the middle of this madness, Jesus Christ comes to them literally walking on the water. He's out on the raging waves in the middle of the storm.

Their first panicked thought—it's a ghost! As if a life threatening storm isn't enough, now we have to deal with evil spirits! But then Jesus calls out to them...

"...*Be of good cheer; it is I; be not afraid*" (Matthew 14:27).

Did he really just say that? In the middle of a chaotic, life-threatening torrent, he calls out a standard picnic greeting—"Be of good cheer!" Really? Be of good cheer? Like—smile, laugh, slap each other on the back, relax, have a good time? In a storm? Hmmm... in a storm Jesus says to experience cheer! Now that's a different take on life for sure.

I believe walking with God through an off script season provides us a rare opportunity to gain a different take on life, on trials, and on what's really important. In all the moments I've described to you—from PET scans to biopsies, to harrowing phone calls, to heart-felt prayers alone—in those moments I had to make a choice. Do I sit down in the face of this storm and just pout and pity myself—expecting everyone else to do the same? Or is there a better way to respond? Is there a greater significance to all this?

And then I read Matthew 14. Not long after Jesus says, "Be of good cheer," He invites Peter out on the water. He tells him to step out of the boat and come to Him. And Peter obeyed. Oh sure, moments later he lost his whits and became fearful of the storm—but he left the boat! Gotta hand it to him! He obeyed.

Off script times are the same with each of us. These are our storms. Our moments to look beyond the emotion, the fear, the harrowing experience and recognize Jesus out on the water. These are our moments to hear Him call to us, "Be happy… it's me… don't be afraid!" Think about that phrase. From the heart of God, He expects us to rest and rejoice with the discovery of His presence. The whole world could be coming to an end, but when we hear "It is I…" we should suddenly have the capacity to be cheerful! The realization should bring relief. It should be cause for celebration!

Cancer?—Oh, but there's God—whew! For a moment there I was scared!

Death? Job loss? Financial setback? Sickness? Sudden tragic turn of events?—Oh, but there's Jesus—whew! For a moment there I was starting to get worried.

More like— "Hey, it's Jesus—time to break into smiles of relief and celebratory laughter! God's in this. He's in control! What a relief—it's all going to be just fine! Jesus is here!"

In the out-of-control times of life, that's what Jesus does. He leads us into the storm, meets us on the water, and shouts, "Hey, be of good cheer; it is I; be not afraid," and then He does the unthinkable. He says, "Come."

In the midst of the storm, He invites you to leave the boat—to leave your sinking symbol of security—to completely abandon your script. He invites you onto the raging water with Him. He encourages you to relinquish your last shred of personal security, to lose your grip on anything you might be holding onto, and risk it all by joining Him in the middle of the chaos. Embrace the storm. Enter into it.

Immerse yourself into the raging waters that harbor the presence of the Almighty. What a mind-blowing proposition. And even more mind-blowing is that Peter actually obeyed!

So here we are—off script and in a storm. Our little boat is useless. This storm is far bigger than any resource at our disposal. We can't save ourselves, buy our way out, or barter for safety. We're toast. Without a miracle, without God, things are pretty bleak. We can bail water, scramble on deck, panic, and generally go nuts. Or we can see Jesus. We can hear Him call out, "Be of good cheer, it is I, be not afraid." And we can make a choice.

What do you do when God rewrites your life?

Here's decision two:

BE OF GOOD CHEER!

See Jesus, be cheerful, refuse to be afraid,
and join Him in the storm.

Easier said than done? Not really. It's just a simple choice that changes the whole experience. It's a decision of the heart, and it's possible. He wouldn't command what we couldn't do. If Jesus invites you to rejoice, then you can. If He tells you not to be afraid, then it can happen. If He expects you to be totally relieved in His presence, then you can be. If he invites you to leave your security and step into the storm, then you must.

Read it again: *See Jesus, be cheerful, refuse to be afraid, and join Him in the storm.*

LET'S BREAK IT DOWN.

It starts with seeing Jesus. When the storm is raging, there's a lot to distract your attention. Your enemy would love nothing more than for you to miss the Master and be utterly overwhelmed by the billows. In chaos it's easy to see nothing but chaos.

When life goes off script, look for Jesus. No matter the threat, no matter the trial—when you see Jesus, everything changes. He is the all-powerful, all-knowing God of the universe. He is bigger than your storm. You must see Him—and you can always find Him in His Word and in your storm.

The second step is to be cheerful. By human rationale, this sounds ridiculous—even ludicrous. How can we be cheerful in the face of such devastating circumstances? Isn't this the time to meltdown? Isn't this the time to descend into depression and self-pity? Isn't this the time to panic and start scrambling for a way out of this mess? But Jesus commanded the disciples to be of good cheer.

Cheer in the midst of hardness is a paradox only possible when you realize that a *joyful* life and an *easy* life are not synonymous. An *easy* life is not always a *happy* life. And a *difficult* life is not always a *sad* life.

Cheer is a product of the presence of God. And in this case, cheer is a deliberate choice of faith. Cheer is more about *Who is in you* than *what is going on around you.* And in this passage, Jesus commanded His followers to be cheerful—not because He had calmed the storm—but because He was there with them.

Off script seasons try to mess with our minds and get us focused on all the wrong things—feeling all the wrong ways. When the raging storm takes center stage in your mind—when you allow your heart to dwell on the grueling nature of your trial, your world becomes anything but cheerful. But when you stop looking at the storm long enough to look to Jesus—when He becomes the center of your focus, cheer becomes a real possibility. Seeing Him in any storm can put a smile back on your face and a calm in your heart, even though the storm is still threatening you!

Don't miss the fact that Jesus *commanded* them to be of good cheer. This was something that they had full cognitive function over. If they remained fearful and anxious, it was their decision. If they expressed cheer, that too was a conscious decision. And so it is with us. You have a choice in your storm—*stress out or cheer up*—and it's very much your choice.

Next, Jesus said "...be not afraid." In some ways these heart changes can happen all at once. For example, seeing Jesus leads to cheer and releases fear. But in other ways, they are conscious steps—deliberate decisions to not let the circumstances dictate your responses.

Personally, as the recent events of my life have unfolded, there have been many moments where fear wanted to call the shots. For the most part it happens when I'm alone, probably most commonly at night. For about the first ninety days of this trial, the only word on my mind every time I would awaken in the night was "lymphoma." It was as if *fear personified* was sitting beside my bed waiting for me to stir, just to shout, "Hey, don't forget, you have lymphoma! What are you gonna do?!" The temptation was to wake up, worry, and in panic think, "What am I doing?! I've got cancer... I don't have time to sleep... I've got to do something!"

In such moments we either listen to fear or we listen to Jesus, and Jesus says, "Be not afraid!" Fear would have kept me up, stewing, wringing my hands, worrying about the future, trying to figure things out. Fear would have choked away sanity, and stability. Fear would have my whole life in tumult and tension.

But when Jesus says, "Be not afraid," He is aiming for calm and stability. He's saying, "Don't be seized with alarm or put to flight with terror." He calls us to refuse the emotion—to reject our tendency to panic. It's a choice. Perhaps it's your choice right now. It's the one choice that will allow you to go back to sleep and let Jesus deal with things you can't!

Finally, Jesus calls Peter to "Come. Join Me on the waves. Step out of the boat and get into the storm." This is more than merely leaving your own security. This is about *accepting* the storm. Think about it.

If I were Peter, I would have tried to strike a deal. "Jesus, why don't You still the storm or at least settle it a bit, then I'll leave the boat. If we're gonna try this impossible 'walk on water thing' let's at least do it on a calmer sea." No, go. Step into the raging, wild, chaotic, and terrifying! What faith and courageous abandon Peter had! What trust!

Even so, I believe there must come a moment when you decide to step into your storm with Jesus. You can stay in the boat wishing He would "do something," but that's not what He's commanding.

Step into the storm. This is the moment when you embrace His script and surrender fully to events He has ordained. This is the moment when you see the storm, not as something to be rescued *from*, but as something to walk *through* with Him. Suddenly the storm is not your torturous taskmaster, but a tool in the hand of your ultimate Master.

The storm of which we read in Matthew 14 is not a random event that Jesus happened to walk into as a participant. This is Jesus, the Almighty, *at the helm* of a storm—the whole thing is in His hand and at His control. The storm is not the center of the story, with Jesus on the sidelines simply stepping in to save the day. Jesus is the *center* of the story, and the storm is His very intent and design.

So it is with your storm. He is at the helm, and He calls us to come into the storm with Him. Now that's a storm we can step into—the one where Jesus is and where He is in complete control!

Once you see Jesus in the storm, it becomes easier to let go of fear, say hello to cheer, and even step out into the mayhem to be near Him.

The presence of God changes everything about your storm.

Yes, your whole world can be caving in around you, way off script, but you can be rejoicing with Jesus as it does. That's the wonder of God's grace and presence in the storm. In essence, you can have a cinnamon roll day even when bone marrow biopsies are on the agenda.

I don't know the details of your off script experience. Frankly, I wish you didn't have one! But I do know you can choose to see Jesus. You can choose to rejoice—to be of good cheer. You can choose to laugh—in abundance and in sincerity. You can choose to enjoy His presence and His strength, even though life has its bitter biopsies. You can choose to step onto the water and walk with Jesus in the midst of the danger. He is waiting for you there. He will meet you there. And only He can make sure this storm doesn't overwhelm your soul.

He wants to be with you.

While the winds and waves rage out of control all around you—*see Jesus, be cheerful, refuse to be afraid, and join Him in the storm.*

I shouldn't have brought up the cinnamon rolls again— my taste buds are demanding a replay of the cinnamon roll ministry!

It Is Well

When peace, like a river, attendeth my way,
When sorrows like sea billows roll;
Whatever my lot, Thou hast taught me to say,
It is well, it is well with my soul.

Though Satan should buffet, though trials should come,
Let this blest assurance control,
That Christ has regarded my helpless estate,
And hath shed His own blood for my soul.

My sin, oh, the bliss of this glorious thought!
My sin, not in part, but the whole,
Is nailed to the cross, and I bear it no more,
Praise the Lord, praise the Lord, O my soul!

And, Lord, haste the day when my faith shall be sight,
The clouds be rolled back as a scroll;
The trump shall resound, and the Lord shall descend,
Even so, it is well with my soul.

—Horatio G. Spafford

THREE
BE THE CLAY

But now, O LORD, thou art our father; we are the clay, and
thou our potter; and we all are the work of thy hand.
—Isaiah 64:8

"YOU HAVE THE LUNGS AND HEART OF AN athlete…." My doctor was giving me the results of the MUGA scan and pulmonary function test. I looked at Dana as if to say, "Be impressed…." She smiled, obviously taken back in feigned amazement. He probably says that to everybody, but I was glad to be cleared for chemo.

As the first week of November passed, we enjoyed a visit from my mom, counted down the days until chemo would begin, and eagerly awaited the final test results—big test results. We were praying for a negative bone marrow biopsy and a PET scan that didn't reveal any surprises or new tumors. The week was relatively unemotional, until we dropped Mom off at the airport on Friday. That's when I was reminded again that this whole ordeal is harder on those who love me than it is on me. I pray for my parents and family frequently.

Hollywood and Gender Confusion

An hour later we arrived at the Kaiser Sunset Hospital—the primary cancer hospital of the Kaiser system located in the "beautiful" cesspool of Hollywood. We were there to see the Radiologist/Oncologist that would determine my radiology treatment. As we waited, we could hear him on the phone in the other room—loudly and confusingly asking other departments for my various test results. A few minutes later, he stepped in, looked straight at Dana, and said, "So, you are Cary Schmidt?"

I forced a smile, looked at Dana, and flatly said, "Yes, I am...."

This was about the fourth time that various doctors and health professionals falsely assumed (because of my name) that I was a woman. This was getting old! My thinking went something like this: "If they aren't even sure of my gender, how are we going to cure cancer?"

Bewildered, he looked at me, then her, then his chart. Awkward pause. "Oh... okay. I guess that could go either way, couldn't it?"

I casually said, "I guess it could..." and forced a smile. Awkward moment continued. Then we all moved on, as

Dana giggled at me once again and patted my shoulder. She really got a kick out of all the gender confusion. God has given us all sorts of humorous moments throughout this off script experience.

The appointment was filled with news—some awesome, and some not so awesome. In many ways the whole day was an experience in juggling two emotional extremes at the same time—extreme delight at the good news, and extreme soberness at the heavy news.

The good news was the bone marrow. The conversation went like this:

Doctor: "So what tests are you still waiting on?"

Me: "Just the bone marrow, but that's not done yet."

Doctor: "Well, it is now… it's negative."

He continued to talk as though he has just said something as mundane as "water is wet," but as for me and Dana—we celebrated! High five! I wanted to jump through the roof! That's huge news! There's no cancer in my bone marrow. This was a wonderful answer to prayer, and I thanked the Lord and wished the doctor would have paused long enough for us to relish the news. But the man was in a hurry. What is it with doctors in a hurry?

Unfavorable News

Only minutes later, the news was a bit heavier. For the first time, this doctor actually pulled up PET scan and CT scan images on screen and explained them to us—showing us every area that was cancerous. Sobering. I had never seen a PET scan image before, but the long story short, it showed a whole lot of cancer in my upper body—a lot more than my other doctors were revealing.

Black tumorous regions showed clearly from the center of my chest across and under my right arm, and another small spot on the left side of my chest. That was the first moment that I had seen for myself what was growing inside me. Suddenly I couldn't wait to start killing it—even if treatment would be difficult.

What I thought was a few swollen lymph nodes in a few regions of my torso actually turned out to be five relatively large areas where clusters of lymph nodes have morphed into bulky masses of cancerous mutiny. The largest of these is actually located on top of my heart and between my lungs, wrapped around my trachea. This explains a lot of my bronchial challenges and energy fluctuations over the last couple of years.

The size of my tumors made my diagnosis "unfavorable"— gotta love these medical terms. I wanted to say, "Isn't the whole situation rather unfavorable?" Ultimately five regions of my upper body are involved, which will require radiation after chemotherapy. My staging was officially 2A, which means we found this cancer relatively early, it's only in my upper body, and I don't have a lot of "B" symptoms. And I made sure, by the time the appointment was over, my health care provider was solid on my gender! Live or die—people better know that I'm a man before this is all over!

That day, the diagnosis was complete, treatment was determined, and we were finally moving ahead to attack this disease. In the words of a friend, "Those lymph nodes are about to get what's coming to them!" I liked that! Game on!

The road ahead would not be easy, but at least I knew what to prepare for. Treatment would include six months of chemotherapy called ABVD. I would receive a treatment every two weeks—twelve in all. After that and some follow-up tests, I would have one month of radiation (twenty daily treatments) during which they would zap all five regions of tumors. The idea being that six months of chemo would radically shrink the tumors and most likely kill all the cancer, and the radiation would wipe out any remaining cells entombed in the tumor scar tissue. Aside from the longterm risks of chemo and radiation, it sounded like a plan to me.

I will never forget two things my doctor told me during the process. The first—"With this cancer, our greatest concern is how to treat you in a way that does the least amount of damage to your body. This cancer has a high rate of cure—we like this one!"

The second—"I'm telling you, you gotta find another way to die. It will not be from this cancer." I appreciated his assurance.

WRESTLING WITH SOVEREIGNTY

By this point in our trial, our heads were spinning. Tests, exams, appointments, treatment schedules, questions, research, and the endless unrelenting voices in the back of my mind—"Hey, don't forget, you have cancer!" In spite of all the news and experiences, physically I felt fine. It was hard to believe something this serious was happening. And it was even harder to try to wrap my brain around the intricacies of God's work in such times.

That's where God's Word comes in. The only place to run, the only place to find sanity and perspective during off script times is the one place where God explains Himself so clearly—His Word. In many ways, the chapters of this book are simply my best effort to take you to the biblical places where God has taken me during this trial—the places in Scripture where He so clearly told me what I needed to know about Himself and His intentions.

In hardship, lots of people ask "Why would God do this? Why would God allow this?" A lot of people have a hard time imagining a good God allowing bad things to happen. But have you ever considered the other side of the argument?

Job was unbelievable! In the words of my good friend, "No wonder he got a whole book!" The man suffered unimaginable loss and pain, and yet he never cursed God. He never questioned God's goodness. He knew God was doing something, but more importantly, He acknowledged God's right to be... well... GOD! He acknowledged God's right to be sovereign—even if that meant difficulty in his own life for reasons beyond his understanding. He understood that God doesn't owe us anything—much less an explanation. Look at his words:

> ...Naked came I out of my mother's womb, and naked shall I return thither: the LORD gave, and the LORD hath taken away; blessed be the name of the LORD. —JOB 1:21

> ...What? shall we receive good at the hand of God, and shall we not receive evil? In all this did not Job sin with his lips.—JOB 2:10

> What is man, that thou shouldest magnify him? and that thou shouldest set thine heart upon him?—JOB 7:17

David sized up man's position with God this way:

> What is man, that thou art mindful of him? and the son of man, that thou visitest him?—PSALM 8:4

> LORD, what is man, that thou takest knowledge of him! or the son of man, that thou makest account of him!—PSALM 144:3

Yes, God is good. Yes, God is love. But, YES, God is sovereign. He is in control, and He warns us that He doesn't think as we think. His ways are not our ways (Isaiah 55:8). God never promises that His doings will always align with our logic or expectations. He doesn't promise to make sense to us. He doesn't owe us a life of ease and pleasure. He doesn't owe us anything. It's beyond belief that He would love us to begin with. It's unthinkable that the Almighty God of the universe would do anything other than destroy us. We are sinful beings who have offended Him, rejected Him, broken His laws, and demanded our own ways.

That's what I am. That's what you are.

Yet this God gave His own Son upon the Cross to save us—shed His perfect blood to redeem us and give us eternal life. When you stand wide-eyed at the Cross and just barely begin to comprehend what took place there because of His great love, that is enough of an answer. No further questions necessary. Cancer? Death? Loss? Heartache? Sorrow? Grief? Well, how dare you God! God, how could you...

The Cross.

Nothing could more loudly say, "God is good, God is love, and anything God chooses to do in your life is acceptable!" Nothing should give God a greater all-time season pass to be God in your life—to do anything and everything He wants to do. Nothing should more release us from requiring any further explanation from our Heavenly Father. The Cross says it all. The Cross is the explanation point that ends every question. The Cross settles every doubt that could ever be aired about God's nature or character.

When you start wrestling with the "whys" and "whats" and "how comes" and "how longs" and all the other endless and unanswerable questions of God's doings, look to Him and you will see Him pointing at the Cross. When the enemy attacks God in your mind and starts demanding Divine explanations—when your heart starts wanting to throw out spiritual ultimatums, commanding God to prove Himself good or to "get you out of the mess He's created"—look again at the Cross.

If God would save you, isn't that beyond all the explanations He could ever offer? Couldn't that be enough for you to say, "In the light of that kind of love, I don't need an explanation."

Why would God allow bad things to happen to good people? Turn it around. *Why would a good God allow good things to happen to bad people.* In our hearts, we know what we deserve—far worse than we experience. Yes, even in allowing hardness in our lives, God is still immeasurably good, loving, gracious, and compassionate.

BE THE CLAY

The morning after our radiology appointment, the Lord woke me up at about 5:30 AM. (I'm normally not that spiritual.) I

resisted for a while, protesting that I needed more sleep—
"Hey, I've got cancer—I need rest!"

But God kept nudging me awake with a different reply,
"Hey, you've got cancer and you need to spend some extra
time with Me. Come see what I'm doing for you!"

About thirty minutes later I stepped out my front door
to the most amazing sunrise I've seen in years. The morning
desert sky was ablaze with light and a radiant spectrum of
colors. It was as if God Himself were standing next to me, big
smile on His face, saying, "How 'bout that!"

It was unreal, and it was one of a hundred ways that God
reminded me of the power and presence of His hand in my
circumstances. I watched the sun come up, talked to Him,
and cherished His presence that morning.

Then He led me to the books of Jeremiah and Isaiah
again where He showed me these words:

> *And the vessel that he made of clay was marred in the
> hand of the potter: so he made it again another vessel, as
> seemed good to the potter to make it.*—JEREMIAH 18:4

> *O house of Israel, cannot I do with you as this potter?
> saith the LORD. Behold, as the clay is in the potter's
> hand, so are ye in mine hand, O house of Israel.*
> —JEREMIAH 18:6

Woe unto him that striveth with his Maker! Let the potsherd strive with the potsherds of the earth. Shall the clay say to him that fashioneth it, What makest thou? or thy work, He hath no hands?—ISAIAH 45:9

But now, O LORD, thou art our father; we are the clay, and thou our potter; and we all are the work of thy hand.—ISAIAH 64:8

Potter and clay. That's the picture. We could spend countless hours on theological exegesis of the sovereignty of God and exactly what that means, and still our human minds would fail us. But this one picture sums it up so simply and perfectly. He is the potter. We are the clay.

Clay doesn't have a will. Clay doesn't expect, presume, or worry. Clay doesn't resist or fight. Clay doesn't have an agenda or a script. Clay has two simple jobs—*sit still and stay soft.*

Recently people have told me that they are angry with God, or that they question God over my situation, or their own. Over the years, I've spent many hours with bitter, frustrated, angry people who have never learned this principle.

Please, my friend. Don't go to the place of anger and bitterness with the Potter. Bring your questions to God, but don't question His nature or His heart. He is God. We are dust. When we question His nature or His goodness, we reveal our frailty and even our arrogance. But when we bring our questions to Him, we find a refuge and a very present help in time of trouble. We find a loving Father!

What do you do when God rewrites your life script?

Decision three:
BE THE CLAY!

Sit still, stay soft, and let God work in your life.

Oh how desperately we want to jump off that potter's wheel and start calling the shots—or run for our lives. When His hands get wrapped around us in a way we don't expect, when He starts reshaping portions of our lives that we are not comfortable with, when He removes something we are clinging to—oh how that hurts, disrupts, and unsettles us. How quickly we want to usurp His work, call a foul, and start acting so "un-clay-like."

What blob of clay ever argued with the potter? What lump ever lept into control? What clod of dirt ever dared to question or accuse the God of the universe? Isn't it amazing that He puts up with us at all?

God wants us to stop the role reversal before it even begins. He reminds us—He's the Potter, we are the clay. The Potter is working and fashioning the clay according to His good pleasure and eternal purpose. The Potter has a master plan that will culminate in ages to come with eternal goodness. Aren't we blessed to be clay in this wonderful Potter's hands!

So, don't jump off the wheel. Don't get dry and crusted with doubt and frustration. Don't allow the enemy to falsely accuse your Potter or bring doubt and unreasonable questions into your heart. Stay still. Stay soft. Let the Potter do His work. *Be the clay.*

Hard to Understand

Let's face it, this is tough stuff—off script times I mean. They are hard to comprehend. They are surreal. And in our control-freakish human tendencies, we want to know. We want to understand. What's going on? Where is this headed? Why is this happening? The questions are endless and in many ways unanswerable. How would a potter explain to a lump of clay what he's really doing?

There's just a lot about our off script moments we can't and won't even begin to grasp until eternity. Knowing "why" isn't nearly as important as resting in the fact that there is a "why." We may not ever get the answers we wish we could have now, but just knowing that the Potter has the answers— well, that's enough.

Probable Outcomes?

So, in closing this chapter, let me speak personally with you about my trial, and yours.

Life is hard. But God is good. Don't confuse the two. Choose not to question God or His sovereign, good hand in your life. Choose to rest in Him. Choose to accept the peace that comes with His purpose.

Life is not merely about survival. It's not about experiencing as many heartbeats as possible. It's not about outlasting other people your age. Too many people live life with two goals—have as many heartbeats as possible, and have as much fun as possible while the heart is beating. This is not wise. Survival, pleasure, and ease are terrible life goals. Aim higher!

Life is all about fulfilling God's purpose and call. It's about being clay in His hands and letting Him fulfill His purpose through you—running your race and finishing your course. That's the only life worth living—even with its hardness and off script experiences.

For instance, my struggle is not about life or death or even cancer; it's about knowing God and fulfilling His call. Cancer is merely a player on the stage of my life right now—just as your circumstances are. Cancer is not a threat, an evil plot, or an assault. More than anything, it's a gift—an instrument or tool in my Potter's hands to do something special in and through me—for His glory and for the benefit of others. (I don't understand how that's all going to happen—I just know God, and that's what He does!) Beating cancer isn't about surviving, and losing to cancer isn't about dying—it's all about fulfilling God's purpose and helping others, like you, to know Him.

Place your hope in the Potter, not in your plans. In my case, the doctors have given me a good prognosis. While I have no guarantees, statistics are on my side. But that doesn't matter if I end up falling into the smaller side of the statistics. And for every eight or nine survival stories I read, I find at least one lost battle against this very cancer. While I will fight hard to live, as the Lord allows, I know my hope isn't found in my odds or in statistics. My hope is in the Potter.

Off script seasons reveal a lot about our lives. Hardship reveals where our hope is found. When your hope is in Christ, hardness doesn't shake that hope; it makes it more secure. Trials reveal our false assumptions. We assume we have longer lives. We assume our hearts should keep beating. We assume our situations are secure. We assume God is something like a "personal genie," keeping all of life healthy, happy, and materially prosperous. When trials surprise us, they can reveal that we were holding onto a lot of false assumptions. And when you think about it, those assumptions are based on nothing more than probability.

Don't live your life clinging to probable outcomes—cling to the Potter. Clinging to probabilities or personal agendas is a sure path to disappointment. Live your life standing solely upon the assurance of God's promises, and the security of His presence. Live knowing that you are His child—clay in His hands. Anything less than the presence and hand of God at work in your life is an illusion—a false assumption.

Remember, He is the potter. Be the clay—sit still, stay soft, and it's all going to work out!

HAVE THINE OWN WAY, LORD

Have Thine own way, Lord! Have Thine own way!
Thou art the potter, I am the clay.
Mold me and make me after Thy will,
While I am waiting, yielded and still.

Have Thine own way, Lord! Have Thine own way!
Search me and try me, Master, today!
Whiter than snow, Lord, wash me just now,
As in Thy presence humbly I bow.

Have Thine own way, Lord! Have Thine own way!
Wounded and weary, help me I pray!
Power, all power, surely is Thine!
Touch me and heal me, Savior divine!

Have Thine own way, Lord! Have Thine own way!
Hold o'er my being absolute sway.
Fill with Thy Spirit till all shall see
Christ only, always, living in me!

—ADELAIDE A. POLLARD

FOUR

CHERISH THE
SECRET PLACES

*And I will give thee the treasures of darkness, and hidden
riches of secret places,* —ISAIAH 45:3

I'M NOT A RUNNER. IN FACT, SINCE MY NINTH
grade year of high school, after a brief and rather unpleasant
season on the track team, I have essentially hated running.
Driving to work each morning in my comfortable and
climate-controlled automobile, I often pass people running.
They are miserable—healthy, yes, but absolutely in torment.

Their body is racked with pain, their lungs are gasping for
breath, the elements are beating their brains out, and their
heart is pounding out of their chest. No thanks.

My definition of health looks more like a glazed donut
and a leather recliner (said the very sickly man). Even the
best jogging shoes, a stylish running suit, and the nicest iPod
armbands do not make the proposition any more attractive.

I'm okay with exercise, but I can think of a lot more happy ways! Running is misery.

But chemo week—I have to be honest with you—I wanted to run. Physically, spiritually, emotionally, mentally—in every way, I wanted away from the overwhelming, horrifying off script place. Give me some running shoes and open road, and get me out of here. Can I leave the country? Can I change my identity? Can I flee this situation in any way? Anywhere but the chemo chair.

The week between the radiology appointment and the beginning of chemo was a flurry of activity and emotions. In my heart and mind, I was partially terrified and wishing I could run. In my family life, I was trying to give Dana and each of the kids quality time and attention—not knowing how the treatment would impact our lives. In ministry life, I tried to work ahead as much as possible in planning meetings with staff teams, not knowing what capacities I would have for work. I felt as if life was going away and wouldn't likely be back until July—though that was no guarantee either.

There was only one place to run—to God and His Word.

D-Day for Cancer Cells

Monday, November 15—D-day for cancer cells and lymph nodes, and one nervous day for our family. We often prayed as a family for healing, strength, and grace. Often at night I would lay awake asking God to help me in this and honor Him. The night before chemo, my last thought was, "tomorrow I'm going to be poisoned...." Strange emotions for sure, but God gave a quiet resolve and calm to my spirit, *"I will be with you."*

We arrived at the medical facility at 9:30 AM where one of our church deacons was waiting (since 8 AM) to hug me and pray with me. What a blessing it was to see him standing there as I walked up the sidewalk to the lab! We hugged and prayed together. Just his presence ministered to my heart in an unspeakable way.

Blood work and a doctor's appointment followed, and by lunch time we were ushered into a room full of chemo chairs and patients. Actually, this was the saddest moment of the whole experience for Dana and me. Seeing all these people getting chemo was hard for us. I'm sure many of them had a much worse prognosis than I did.

I've never been comfortable sitting in a chair if my feet can't touch the ground. But that's where I ended up—in a large green chair, feeling like an eight-year-old sent to the principal's office. It was covered in vinyl and sort of "hospital-ish"—wheels and all—not the chair I would watch a football game from for sure. Dana sat in front of me and we just stared at each other—rather unsure of our emotions. She tried to look strong and supportive—and happy, but I think we were both at about 9.7 on the nervousness richter scale. We knew life was about to change—dramatically.

After having the IV hooked up, I waited for my personal poison to arrive—two bags of pre-medications followed by three slow injections and a final fluid bag, all given over about five hours. In the middle of it all, we met with a pharmacist who gave us a boatload of other instructions about all the other medications required between treatments. The number of different medications and pills was mind-boggling. We took lots of notes.

Finally by about 4 PM I left the doctor's office both highly toxic and heavily drugged. Now it was all about waiting to get sick—which was only a few hours away.

The Cancer-Cell Apocalypse

This is weird, but my brain has a rather comical (some say "warped") way of processing these experiences. The first day of treatment, I had a sort of movie script playing out in my brain. It went something like this:

Scene one—cancer cells (I give them personalities in my mind) bad characters—smoking, drinking, playing cards, hanging out in lymph node bars, multiplying and dividing, and just being cancerous. They hang out in masses and generally create trouble.

Scene two—suddenly, (cue epic music, and put a sudden and surprised look on all their faces) all mayhem breaks loose! Chemo is coming! They panic. Then they start screaming, flinging their cigars and cards in every direction, and running for their lives—"Head for the kidneys! Every man for himself! AHHHH!" (Music builds as cells are overtaken and destroyed...)

Scene three—lymph node night-clubs are shut down and turned into local churches and community service centers as normalcy and revival returns to the immune system. (Cue happy ending music...)

Throughout treatment, I have replayed that movie in my mind many times. It definitely helps with the sickness, and it's always good to think about those cancer cells dying and lymph nodes being given a major attitude adjustment!

MAJOR BUMMER

Leaving the chemo room that day, I experienced a major disappointment and, frankly, uncovered a massive oversight in the medical industry.

Dozens of times in my life I have experienced dental or orthodontic trauma—like fillings, tooth-pullings, and root-canals, but these experiences always ended with a long-anticipated trip to a treasure chest filled with great toys. If you were good during treatment, you get to pick one toy. If you were *really* good during treatment, you get to pick two. And if you happen to have a nurse with an unusual level of renegade kindness, she would turn the other way and let you sneak three toys or more—acting like she didn't see!

Picking the treasure at the end of the trauma was like the light at the end of the dental-drill tunnel! Sweet relief! No matter that you were still bleeding heavily into a piece of saliva-saturated, well-bitten cotton gauze. No matter that your face was still numb and sliding off your skull, or that your brain was still slap-happy from goofy gas. No matter. The treasure chest was a most cherished and delightful destination. A sort of "rite of passage" for having endured the anguish of dental torture.

Well, if there's any place in America where there ought to be a very well-stocked treasure chest, extremely generous nurses, and highly valuable treasures from which to choose—it's the chemo room! It ought to be the largest piece of furniture in the room, visible to every chair, and softly calling your name during your whole infusion! And so I asked my nurse—"You guys got a treasure chest around here if I'm good?" She just laughed. I was serious.

No treasure chest? In the chemo room of all places? This is tragic.

TREASURES OF DARKNESS

In retrospect, the treasures of the dental office—you know, little plastic army men with parachutes, spinners, yo-yos, dart-guns—weren't really all that great. It was probably the remnant effect of the goofy gas that gave them such an aura of radiance in my childhood brain. But compared to the torment of the dentist chair, they were rich and precious treasures of sweet relief!

Wouldn't it be really cool if God had a treasure chest? If the dark places of our lives involved a stop-over of rewards somewhere along the experience?

Good news! He does!

Your Heavenly Father has not left your dark place without treasures of wonderful relief—hidden riches of blessing, strength, and grace. He has designed your dark place to also be a place of richness and reward. He has planned this "experience in anguish" to also involve intimate moments of sacred delight. He desires to walk with you in secret places, to reveal to you hidden riches, to lavish you with treasures that are only found in the dark places of life.

In Isaiah chapter 45 we read these words:

> Thus saith the LORD to his anointed, to Cyrus, whose right hand I have holden, to subdue nations before him; and I will loose the loins of kings, to open before him the two leaved gates; and the gates shall not be shut; I will go before thee, and make the crooked places straight: I will break in pieces the gates of brass, and cut in sunder the bars of iron: And I will give thee the treasures of darkness, and hidden riches of secret places, that thou mayest know that I, the LORD, which call thee by thy name, am the God of Israel. For Jacob my

servant's sake, and Israel mine elect, I have even called thee by thy name: I have surnamed thee, though thou hast not known me. I am the LORD, and there is none else, there is no God beside me: I girded thee, though thou hast not known me: That they may know from the rising of the sun, and from the west, that there is none beside me. I am the LORD, and there is none else.
—Isaiah 45:1–6

There's a long story and a lot of history here, so let me summarize it briefly for you.

The nation of Israel is being prepared for a time in captivity and exile, and God chose a man named Isaiah to be one of His prophets to preach His message to the people of Israel. When we arrive in chapter 45, God is about to predict events that were still two centuries away. With amazing providential detail He describes a ruler named Cyrus whom He would one day anoint for a particular purpose. He says to Cyrus, who isn't even born yet, "I'm going to hold your right hand and subdue nations and kings before you. I will break down defenses that stand in your way. I will go before you to prepare and straighten the path."

And then God promises to give Cyrus the "treasures of darkness" and "hidden riches of secret places." What is He referring to?

In the grand scheme, big-picture, God is revealing Himself to mankind. In verse 6 He makes that clear. From the east (the rising of the sun) to the west—that they (all the people of the earth) may know *that there is none beside me. I am the LORD, and there is none else.* " God, in all of His dealings with Israel throughout all of Scripture, is fully engaged in His redemptive work for the human race—calling all of humanity to Himself. He is using Israel to reveal Himself to us—just as He desires to use you to reveal Himself to others. He is showing us and reminding us over and over again through biblical events that He is the only God and there is none else. He is our only hope.

In this chapter, we simply step into a moment in God's plan for the ages—just one scene in the middle of His grand story. At this moment, Cyrus is His chosen vessel—in *your* moment, *you are.* And basically God is saying to Cyrus, "In about 130 years, I'm going to send the nation of Israel into captivity in Babylon. Among them, some will love Me and remain faithful to Me, and I will be with them. I will uphold them and care for them and provide for them. In the middle of that I'm going to anoint you—Cyrus—to overtake the Babylonian Empire and then use you to free the nation of Israel to return to their home and rebuild their lives."

Specifically, His promise to Cyrus in this chapter is that he would be undefeatable until he had completed his mission for God. And His promise was to lead Cyrus, to guide him, to prepare the way for him, and to give him hidden treasures and secret riches.

What does this mean? And more specifically what does this have to do with the off script places in our lives?

For Cyrus it meant that all the hidden wealth and riches of the kingdom of Babylon—which was significant—would become His. All the bounty taken from the regions Babylon had conquered would eventually fall to Cyrus' possession. God was going to take Cyrus on a journey—a predetermined destiny—in which God was preeminent. It was a victorious journey that would be filled with supernatural intervention and divinely provided treasure. And this all would result in God unquestionably being glorified and exalted as the one true and only God of all.

For the nation of Israel it meant that even in the darkness of exile and captivity, God would not forget them. All the riches and treasures of the temple that were once stolen, desecrated, and carried into Babylon, would eventually return to the nation of Israel under God's divine providence and direction. God's hand was upon them, with them, before them, and upholding them—even when they least suspected it. Even when they were most certain that God had completely abandoned them, He would be with them.

Imagine being King Cyrus and reading your story—your very name—in the book of Isaiah written two hundred years prior! In the first few verses of Ezra 1 you can read his own words. He figured it out, and he obeyed God. He did indeed discover the treasures of darkness and the hidden riches of secret places. But I believe the greatest treasure he discovered was not the golden artifacts of the darkened vaults and secret places of Babylon. The greatest treasure he discovered was the Almighty God of Heaven and His providential plan for Cyrus.

Stepping into the Secret Places

What does all this mean for you? How does this impact your dark place? What do these complex, historical events reveal to us about the nature of the God of the Universe that we call our "Heavenly Father"?

So much. More than could be written here. I pause overwhelmed at the scope and struggling to find a point in this treasure chest where the Lord might have me dip this pen and begin to write. For truly, this is a vast, unfathomable treasure chest of the unspeakable riches of the goodness and graciousness of your great God.

Like Cyrus, God has chosen you—*anointed* you—to walk this path. It is a part of His plan and purpose. It is a vital thread woven into the broader tapestry of His immense providential plan for the ages. It is a process that will allow God to reveal Himself, to glorify Himself, and to show Himself to you and to others through you. It is *you* on an eternal mission with God, for His ultimate glory.

As with Cyrus, God wants to walk with you in your darkness. He wants to hold your hand. He wants to go before you and prepare the way. He wants to take that which is crooked— the twisted, uncertain, confounded paths—and make them straight before you. He wants to give you clarity amidst the confusion and direction in the middle of desperation.

As with Cyrus, God wants to sustain and protect you in this journey. He will pull down and flatten the things that intimidate you. He will break apart that which terrifies you. He will debilitate your adversary, disable obstructions, and defuse your opposition. *He will render your enemy incapable of using your trial against you.* He will insure that you, His chosen vessel, accomplish all that He has ordained and that you possess all you need to persevere.

As with Cyrus, God then desires to take your hand and bring you into dark places that He might reveal treasures you've never seen—valuable things you never knew existed. He desires to lead you into secret places where He will bless you with hidden riches and pour out upon you blessings that few have ever experienced.

You cannot experience the treasures of darkness unless you are willing to enter that darkness with God Himself.

In off script places, God extends His hand and says, "Grab ahold." God invites you to step into secret places. He leads you through the darkness where He reveals Himself to be *the greatest treasure*. He doesn't *send* you into a trial—He *leads* you into it. He has gone before you. There is no place to step where He has not already stepped. There is no bend in the road that He has not already straightened.

Just as He was the center of the storm for Peter, He is the center of your darkness—the center of your whole destiny. It's all about Him, and in this dark and difficult time, He has chosen *you* to glorify His name among people who need to know Him.

What do you do when God rewrites your script?

Decision four:
CHERISH THE SECRET PLACES

Walk with God in private moments. Cherish the treasure of His presence in the darkness of life.

FINDING YOUR WAY IN THE DARK

Have you ever tried to navigate darkness without a light? It's impossible! You can try to get around, but it's pointless. And darkness is even worse if you're looking for something specific—like valuable treasure.

Even so, the dark journeys of life are hopeless without a very real, intimate, and personal walk with God. Holding His hand and trusting His light, you discover something amazing. *He is* the treasure of the darkness. *He* is the hidden riches of secret places. His presence, His perspective, His promises are the greatest discovery in all of life, but sometimes it takes darkness for us to see Him with clarity.

Walking with Him, discovering Him, knowing Him—these experiences make the darkness disappear and the suffering subside. These things make the journey through difficulty worth taking. These things truly are the treasure chest in the midst of the trial!

As you venture through your off script experience, many may pray for you. Many may encourage you. Many may reach out to bless you. And you will thank God for each and every person who does so. But no one can be God for you. No one can walk with God for you. No one can make you enter His presence and hold onto His hand. This is something only you can choose to do.

There are many that endure hardships and suffering in life. But only a few who reach into the darkness to hold God's unseen hand. Few are those who genuinely find the treasures of darkness and the hidden riches of secret places in Him.

WALKING WITH GOD

Allow me to finish this chapter with a very practical plea
that I pray will lead you into a private, intimate, and
personal walk with God through your darkness.

You will find God in His Word. I'm not writing about
some mystical spiritual experience. I'm writing about a very
deliberate choice to open God's Word and meet Him there.

There is no formula for this walk. You may do it daily. You
may do it every now and then. The more the better. It should
not be rushed or mechanical. It should not be restrained. It
should be you, in quiet, uninterrupted moments, looking
into the Word of God with a tender and focused heart. You
should not be burdened with text messages, emails, or other
disruptions that demand attention. You should lock out the
world, quiet your soul, and open the living Word.

God is on every page. His heart is in every line. His character
and nature woven into every paragraph. His promises are
in every chapter. It doesn't matter where you read so long
as you look for God and listen to Him speak to your heart.
He will. He will absolutely meet you there and minister to
you. This is not about fulfilling a duty, checking off a task,
or impressing another with your spiritual discipline. This is
not about religious ritual or the science of Christian living.
It is about a relationship—pure, simple, intimate, abundant,
and unrestrained.

As Jesus invites in Revelation 3:20—when you open this door, He will come in, sit down, and one on one, sup with you—commune with you personally and privately. You will look into His eyes and He will look into yours. It will forever change your life.

God knows every detail of your situation. He knows every imagination of your heart. He understands every one of the thousands of emotions you feel. He is intimately acquainted with you—right now, right where you are on every level of life. And through His Word, He will speak. He will guide you, minister to you, grow you, transform you. He will give you grace, strength, joy, and hope. He will remind you of Who He is, what He is doing, how He works, and where you are in His care. He will teach you how to respond, how to feel, how to think, and how to step forward. He will assure you, uphold you, and unburden you. He will meet you in His Word, and you will discover all over again, every time, just how awesome He truly is.

You won't necessarily know that all this is happening—but you will know that God is there and working in you. You will sense His reality and His presence. You will be aware that something uniquely Divine is unfolding within you by His Spirit.

Equip yourself with study helps—a concordance, perhaps a dictionary, perhaps a commentary of the Bible like Matthew Henry's (available for free online as well). Understand what you are reading. Seek out the definitions of words, the context of passages, the historical surroundings of books of the Bible. And in it all, seek God and ask Him to reveal Himself to you. He will not fail to speak to you in this moment in life—to give you exactly what you need.

Write down and share what He teaches you. You would be wise to do this with a pen in hand and journal open. He will certainly speak in ways that you wish to remember and pass along to others.

In these moments God will strengthen your heart. He will change your perspective and infuse your soul with gratitude and hope. He will fill you with the joy of His presence, the light of His countenance, the power of His Spirit. He will transform you from within in ways that nothing else in life ever could. He will provide for you the things that no one else could. There is no replacement for the time you spend alone with God in His Word.

I warn you—it's addicting. Time with God fills a longing in your soul that only He can fill. The more you meet God in solitude during the dark times of life, the more of God you will crave. The more you experience these treasures of darkness, the more you will long to retreat from the activity of life and cherish the secret places again with God. These places, these treasures will become the things in life you most value. And while you will be required to pull away from the secret places and re-enter life, you will miss the secret place with God alone.

As you go about your day—working, serving, expending, and living in all the ways you normally do, there will be a deep burning, longing, and hunger in your soul that never ceases, never pauses—calling you back to the secret place with your Heavenly Father. If you ignore it, it will grow quieter and the noise of life can drown it out. But when the busyness of life can finally be stilled again, and you return to the secret place, your soul will revive once again. Your heart will delight like it never does in any other context. There's nothing like drinking living water and tasting the bread of life from the Word of God.

Your darkness was not meant to blind you. It was meant to open your eyes to things that lightness masks. It was meant to reveal to you the treasures of God's heart that only darkness and secret places can unveil. Your trial was not designed to destroy you. It was designed to deliver you into the presence of the one true God who longs to make Himself known to you on a very personal and intimate level.

When you meet God in the secret places, your life is never the same. Your trial is never the same. Your perspective is never the same. Your expectations are never the same.

Come healing or death. Come financial peace or destruction. Come deliverance or exile. Come acceptance or rejection. *The significance of difficult circumstances diminish greatly in the presence of God.* The hope of any specific expected outcome withers into relative obscurity.

The God of the Universe has met me here. No petty treasure of healing, wholeness, prosperity, or earthly benefit could possibly compare to the monumental treasure of knowing Him, being upheld by Him, and fulfilling His call upon my otherwise nothing life. In His presence, the outcome of my trial matters not. He is all and in all. His purpose is all that matters. His glory is the supreme consequence. There is no treasure greater than He is.

If you do not walk with God, you are wasting your trial. If you do not discover Him, your trial will eventually win. You will lose the fight to despair, hopelessness, and failed human reasoning. If you do not meet Him in the secret places, you are condemned to suffer alone in the limits of human logic and fleshly perspective. The power of positive thinking is not enough. Only the presence of the Almighty will genuinely and abundantly strengthen your heart.

People who know God—they will glance your way with a knowing smile as if to say, "You're getting in on the treasure!" People who know of Him but don't know Him will question, "How... why... are you able to cope?" People who don't know God will silently wonder and wish to know this God as you do!

THE TREASURE CHEST

I would rather have one hundred root canals than one more chemotherapy treatment. I know what you're thinking—no, it's not about the dentist's treasure chest! Although, a hundred little plastic army men with parachutes—now that would be a lot of fun on a windy day. Hmmm…

Honestly, cancer is horrible. Chemotherapy is extra-horrible. And the fact that medical providers have completely overlooked the treasure chest in the chemo room only adds insult to injury. Something should be done about this—absolutely. It's a tragic and unfortunate oversight.

But I have discovered God's wonderful treasure chest and the riches of walking with Him through dark places. The presence of God and time with Him is filled with the treasures of His grace. It is abundant and overflowing with the hidden riches of His heart. But it is found only when you hold His hand and walk with Him into the darkness of secret places. No one can lead you to His treasure chest but Him!

Please don't let the darkness overwhelm you. Silence your world, still your soul, reach for God's hand, open His Word, and meet Him. Walk with Him. Sup with Him. Look into His eyes and let Him try your heart. Truly, you will find the treasures of darkness and the hidden riches of secret places.

Go ahead Cyrus—God is calling. God has chosen you—*anointed* you to walk this journey. He goes before you. There is vast, undiscovered treasure to claim. There is a providential eternal purpose to fulfill. There is a God to reveal to people who need to know Him.

You must know Him so that you can make Him known. How about right now?

Grab His hand and cherish the secret places with Him!

SPEAK, O LORD

Speak, O Lord, as we come to You
To receive the food of Your Holy Word.
Take Your truth, plant it deep in us;
Shape and fashion us in Your likeness,
That the light of Christ might be seen today
In our acts of love and our deeds of faith.
Speak, O Lord, and fulfill in us
All Your purposes for Your glory.

Teach us, Lord, full obedience,
Holy reverence, true humility;
Test our thoughts and our attitudes
In the radiance of Your purity.
Cause our faith to rise; cause our eyes to see
Your majestic love and authority.
Words of pow'r that can never fail—
Let their truth prevail over unbelief.

Speak, O Lord, and renew our minds;
Help us grasp the heights of Your plans for us—
Truths unchanged from the dawn of time
That will echo down through eternity.
And by grace we'll stand on Your promises,
And by faith we'll walk as You walk with us.
Speak, O Lord, till Your church is built
And the earth is filled with Your glory.

—STUART TOWNEND AND KEITH GETTY

A Personal Relationship with Jesus Christ

Perhaps, as you're reading these pages, you've come to realize that you do not have a personal relationship with Jesus Christ. Perhaps the very purpose of your off script season is to bring you to the moment when you trust Christ as your personal Saviour. He truly is the treasure of darkness, and choosing Him is the most important decision you could ever make in this life.

His death on the Cross provides the payment for our sin, and His love offers us eternal life. God's Word says "That if thou shalt confess with thy mouth the Lord Jesus, and shalt believe in thine heart that God hath raised him from the dead, thou shalt be saved. For with the heart man believeth unto righteousness; and with the mouth confession is made unto salvation" (Romans 10:9–10).

If you've never made this decision, then I encourage you to do so right now. With your whole heart, choose to believe in Jesus Christ as the only Son of God and sacrifice for your sins. Then, simply pray and invite Him to come into your life and be your Saviour. He will answer this prayer, come into your life, and give you His gift of eternal life. There is no greater decision and no greater assurance than knowing Jesus Christ as Saviour.

If you would like to read more about this relationship with Christ, I encourage you to download the free e-book that I wrote called *Done*.

You will find it at this link in several languages and in audio format as well: www.caryschmidt.com/done

FIVE
WALK IN THE SPIRIT

Know ye not, that to whom ye yield yourselves servants to obey, his servants ye are to whom ye obey;—ROMANS 6:16

EARLY INTO THE CHEMO EXPERIENCE I SAT DOWN and made a list of possible reasons that I contracted Hodgkin's. Though no one really knows what causes it, I have a few suspicions of my own:

I'm a Dallas Cowboys fan. This is the fault of a family in our church who lured my boys astray years ago. I was just trying to be a supportive father, but I fear it was a bad decision.

My parents poisoned me when I was a kid. My brothers and I have had long standing suspicions that our parents conspired against us as children in a multitude of ways, yet every time we foiled their plan and survived. This could have been some "time-release" plot on their part.

The global elite identified me as a threat. It occurred to me that those forming the new world order may have decided they don't want me around, so they tainted my flu shot. Or perhaps I'm involved in a population control plan.

I'm a test case for a bio-terrorism group. Another possible conspiracy explanation.

I'm a youth pastor and teenagers are toxic. I knew youth ministry was risky, but had no idea there were such health sacrifices. Perhaps in families or smaller quantities teenagers are harmless, but in large doses they become lethal?

My absorbed twin is trying to get me back. Perhaps somewhere in my genetics my long lost, previously unknown, absorbed twin is still fighting for survival and found a way to fight back.

Too much pizza over the last twenty-one years. Every one knows the fast food pizza places don't use real ingredients, right? Just chemicals and stuff? So maybe youth ministry strikes again.

Only extremely good-looking and intelligent people get it. I read this on a lymphoma support blog, and it made a lot of sense. When I read it out loud my wife said, "Naaa… that's definitely not it." Her spiritual gift is encouragement.

My body disagrees with my lifestyle and wants out of the deal. Obviously my lymph nodes decided to mutiny.

I'm getting what was promised for not forwarding a couple of those chain emails. You know, the ones that say something bad will happen unless you forward it to everyone you know.

Chemo makers saw a dip in sales and drew my name. Maybe there's a central sickness lottery controlled by the medical elite and a secret "illness distribution system" for the winners.

I live in a desert that was used for nuclear testing. This would explain other oddities about me, and especially my children!

Ups and Downs of Treatment

My first chemo treatment brought sickness for a few days, but wore off soon enough and God allowed us to have a wonderful family Thanksgiving. I could even taste the food! What a blessing.

Each morning brought with it a choice—I will spend this day crying or laughing—moping or rejoicing. Since I love to laugh, and my nose runs more when I cry, I lean toward laughter.

This is not to say that all tears represent despair or self-pity—for the difficult times of life surely involve tears of anguish and release—especially in moments of surrender and transparency before the Lord, or in tender moments with family and friends. It's okay to cry. God tells us in Psalm 56:8 that He is attentive to our tears, "Thou tellest my wanderings: put thou my tears into thy bottle: *are they* not in thy book?"

The cancer journey in anyone's life would certainly fill a few bottles with tears.

One thing is certain, despair is a choice just as happiness is a choice. Each is an act of the will. The first is a decision to be the hostage of fear and circumstances, the second is a choice to embrace the faith life. Tears don't have to equal discouragement or depression. And dark times in life don't have to lead us into self-pity and reclusion.

But this is a moment by moment choice. If I let the hardship and emotions have their way, I will descend into self-pity, depression, and eventually bitterness. That would be dumber than a lump of clay. But if I acknowledge God's hand and choose to rejoice and rest in Him, the joy of the Lord will be my strength. That would be more "clay-like."

Even so, daily, with the rising of the sun, you will face the same decision in your trial. The hardship and your emotions will remind you to be discouraged. But the Holy Spirit will remind you to "be of good cheer." And you must choose your response.

Chemo is a really wonderful, horrible invention! On one level, praise the Lord for granting humanity the wisdom and ability to invent chemicals that kill one kind of cell without killing your whole body. Thank you, Lord, for these chemicals that kill cancer, extend life, and allow a cure in many cases. On another level, these chemicals are pure poison that take your body, brain, and emotions on a vicious voyage like no other.

My chemo assignment involves twelve chemo treatments spaced two weeks apart. So the Monday after Thanksgiving was meant to be my second treatment, but no go. My blood work came back, in the words of the nurse, "Abnormal." You gotta love these medical terms that just leave you hanging. I'm abnormal? Tell me something my family doesn't already know! Will somebody please tell me what *abnormal* means.

Then the doctor walked in, speaking again in that awesome Nigerian accent, "Your white blood cell count dropped like a rock! This I did not expect from you. I tend to think of you as Superman." (He was referring to the bent needle biopsy.)

Trying to cover for my apparent blood flaw I said, "Well, yes, in most cases that is true, but apparently not in white blood cell count."

We both laughed, but then he proceeded to tell me that I could not have treatment that day. No chemo? That's awesome! Postponed treatment? Not so awesome. And then more bad news—something called *Neupogen*. I would have to take yet another medication to promote the growth of white blood cells. I asked if glazed donuts would help, but apparently FDA has not approved that course of treatment yet.

I really hate shots. Needles are not my friends. They rank with snakes in the "ferocious hatred" category of my mind. What a joy to find out that Neupogen is given by self-administered injection—a fancy way of saying, "You gotta learn to give yourself shots." (And all the diabetics are thinking, *you wimp!*) For seven days in a row, after chemo, I would be required to take a small vile of clear liquid each evening, draw it into a syringe, and inject it into my gut. The nurse gave me a quick lesson, a large box of needles, some alcohol wipes, and sent me on my merry way.

"Why so many needles?" I asked on my way out the door.

"Because you're going to be doing this after every chemo treatment for the next six months—you're going to need them." Bummer. Significant bummer.

I looked at Dana, she winced at me, and so began a ritual that I have truly come to loathe. I have developed the convenient habit of forgetting my shot every night, but Dana has developed the tenacious and rather annoying habit of handing it to me with a firm, "You have to take your shot tonight."

One night, I was overwhelmed. I couldn't do it again. It was too much. Something welled up within me with firm resolved resistance. *I'm not doing this tonight. I'm taking the night off of shots!* So I put the stuff away, made Dana think I took the shot, then snuck back downstairs and put the little vile back into the refrigerator.

As soon as I stepped back into the bedroom she said, "What are you doing?!" I tried to look innocent, but those experienced-mother instincts were onto me like white on rice. I was busted and I knew it—and the look on my face totally exposed my malice! I confessed, immediately pleaded for relief, and fortunately her mercy prevailed that night. We never told the doctor.

About the time that the many side-effects of the chemo and related medications start wearing off, the side-effects of Neupogen kick-in. It's like chemo says, "Okay, I'm clocking out," and Neupogen says, "Okay, I'm here for second shift!" This made the six-day recovery from chemo more like an eleven day recovery—and just about the time I was feeling functional again, Monday would roll around and it was time for another treatment.

Now, whenever a happy thought comes into my brain, a sad thought stands up and shouts, "Yeah... but Monday's coming!" It's a savage battle of emotions at times.

Neupogen side effects include some nausea, dry-cough, and primarily bone pain. The chemical finds its way to the bone marrow where it says, "Hey guys, get busy—we need to triple production of white cells this week." So a few days into the shots, the bones start hurting like nothing I've ever felt before. And coughing or sneezing really kicks it up a notch.

The good news is, the pain means white cells are growing and the immune system is coming back online. And after a couple of days, the pain subsides. And fortunately, a few treatments in, I was able to negotiate with the doctor to lower the number of shots depending on my blood counts. As of this writing, I'm bouncing between four and five.

THE PRECIOUS PORTACATH

The week after Thanksgiving held another new experience in this off script adventure. I was advised to have a portacath implanted into my chest. This is a small device that allows the chemo infusion to be administered directly into a larger vein in the chest so that the chemo chemicals don't damage the veins in the arm over time.

I made the mistake of not reading much information about this until the night before surgery. Then I made the mistake of reading about it! Ironically the first four Google results I read were like the world's greatest collection of portacath horror stories—infections, surgeons in training, wrong vein, wrong anesthesia, wrong placement, re-installations, lung punctures, pain, and more. It was actually bizarre. All I did was search "portacath," and WHAM! Suddenly, I'm sweating and ready to cancel surgery! Then I started laughing—*this is too crazy*, I thought. The devil is trying to scare me.

So, I decided to add some "happy words" to my search—like "glad" and "awesome"—hoping there was a happy land of portacath stories out there. Indeed, I found some good accounts. I actually considered having two installed—high on each side of my neck so I would look like Frankenstein. Dana voted no on that.

About 8:15 the next morning, Dana kissed me and I was rolled into an operating room in Hollywood. For the next forty-five minutes two guys prep'd the room and me in a variety of ways—finally covering me with a large blue plastic sheet, including most of my face. By about 9 AM, the surgeon came in and the procedure began.

I had a mixture of emotions to find out I would be awake during the surgery. And thirty minutes later the surgeon is tugging and pulling and says, "You have really thick skin." I'm laying there trying to process it all and wondering ...*what do you say to that?...thanks?*

Forty-five minutes later I was wheeled off to a recovery room where I spent the next two hours sipping orange juice and asking nurses to either bring my wife in or "break me out"—to no avail.

By noon, we were leaving the hospital and I generally felt like someone had crammed some coffee straws inside of my chest, along with the round end of a small stethoscope, and drugged me heavily. The soreness wore off over the following few days, and I have come to love and hate the port. It makes treatments easier, but I'm counting the days until it will be removed. There had better be a treasure chest in that recovery room!

The great blessing of the portacath experience? For the first time, I was listed as *male* on my medical chart. Finally these people knew I was a man. Somehow that made the whole experience a bit more bearable.

Ups and Downs

Congratulations for sticking with me through this chapter. I hope you're laughing some. The point of all this is simply— the off script times of our lives are like roller coaster rides of emotions. It's a roller coaster you've never ridden before, and the track is in the dark so you have no way of knowing where it's all headed. The twists and turns and ups and downs are completely unpredictable and seemingly out of nowhere. They jerk you around like a dish-rag in a dryer. The main difference between this and a roller coaster? This ride isn't fun, and it's definitely not one you're going to get back in line for!

Trials can be horrible emotional experiences. One day you're processing heavy news, the next you're holding onto the smallest bit of good news. One day you're weeping your heart out and the next you're laughing your head off. The chemo experience is almost a moment to moment exercise in evaluating whether you can function or not. One moment you're starting to feel better and beginning to have mental clarity, the next moment you're in a dark cave completely unable to function.

Ups and downs. Off script times can feel completely out of control. Thankfully those are just emotions talking—and emotions aren't running this show. Or they shouldn't be. Let's dig a little deeper into this mess of emotional peaks and valleys and discover what to do with it all.

The Spirit vs. the Emotions

God's Word tells us in Daniel 6:3, "Then this Daniel was preferred above the presidents and princes, because an excellent spirit was in him; and the king thought to set him over the whole realm." Again there's a lot of history here.

Daniel was a young man when the nation of Israel was overtaken by the kingdom of Babylon and a pagan king named Nebuchadnezzar. He had grown up hearing the preaching of God's prophets like Jeremiah, and apparently he had received their message. The prophets had prepared the people that captivity was coming, it was unavoidable, and God's intent was that they should submit to their captors, enter captivity, and continue to honor and love God through it all. God's promise was, for those who would remain faithful during captivity, He would be with them and would care for them, and eventually He would bring them back home.

If anyone ever had a good reason to complain or mope, it would have been Daniel. He was a God-loving young man whose life was suddenly and irreversibly taken off script by a pagan king. Yet, Daniel knew these unpleasant, earth-shaking events were determined by the providence of Almighty God. He looked beyond the circumstances and human players and saw the Divine. He saw the hand of God and chose to honor God rather than reject Him.

One of the many decisions Daniel made was to allow God to rule his spirit. This is why the Bible declares Daniel to be a man with an "excellent spirit." He was excessive, exceedingly above and beyond the norm when it came to his attitude and his heart.

God's Word says in Proverbs 16:32, "He that is slow to anger is better than the mighty; and he that ruleth his spirit than he that taketh a city." The word *rule* refers to having control of or dominion over. And the word *spirit* refers to the source of your disposition.

Your spirit, when you were saved, became the point of rebirth—that part of your being that was indwelled by the Holy Spirit of God. And at that moment, you were given the very presence of God in your life as the source of your being. The fountain head of all personality traits and dispositional qualities was made new in Christ—you became a new creature (2 Corinthians 5:17).

Most people go through life completely controlled by their emotions and their flesh. Like a large dog walking a small child, the emotions and flesh jerk us around with rabid unpredictability. But salvation in Christ changes all of that— potentially. The presence of the Holy Spirit of God makes the mind of Christ, the life of Christ, the emotions of Christ available to our frail humanity. Because the Holy Spirit lives within, you now have the potential to bring your emotions into the control of a Higher Authority.

There's a huge difference between your *emotions* and your *spirit*. And as a side note, I can't pretend to have a complete grasp of the human spirit as it intertwines with the Holy Spirit of God. It's a very practical reality, but also an unexplainable complexity that Scripture doesn't precisely break down. The truth remains, your human emotions are not purely equivalent to your spirit or to God's Spirit that dwells within you.

In Galatians 5:16 God says, "This I say then, Walk in the Spirit, and ye shall not fulfil the lust of the flesh." Ephesians 5:18 commands us to "be filled with the Spirit." And again, in Galatians 5:25 we are instructed, "If we live in the Spirit, let us also walk in the Spirit."

These verses point us to the truth that the Holy Spirit of God desires to rule our human spirit and dictate our emotions and responses. Your human emotions can develop a mind of their own and can lead you far from God's desired responses in your life. But the Holy Spirit of God, when allowed to, will reign in those emotions and control them—bringing about a completely different set of responses to life's storms.

Early into my cancer experience the difference between my spirit and my emotions became crystal clear. From the first news of cancer, my emotions started yanking my chain like a dog on a leash trying to break free to chase a stray cat or random bird. Emotions quickly grasped for control. They wanted to keep me awake, cause my mind to race, scream at me to fear, and generally wreak havoc in my heart. They consistently lied to me, taunted me, and tried to lead me into the mire of self-pity and depression.

Yet, to a greater degree, from the first difficult moment, God's Spirit began speaking calm and composure. In my spirit I knew that God was drawing me and compelling me to yield my emotions to Him, rather than letting them run awry. It was a very real and very moment-by-moment battle. Emotions would try to rise up, but God's Spirit would reach out for the leash and force them back into submission.

I can't say that God's Spirit has won every battle in this journey. There have been moments when discouragement and self-pity seemed to get the best of me. But I can say that the difference between emotions and God's Spirit has never been more clear. And the experience of allowing emotions to be controlled by God's Spirit has never been a more practical, real dynamic through every moment of every day.

YIELD TO THE SPIRIT

The off script times present a very real battle—the Spirit versus the emotions. The roller coaster ride is violent, unpredictable, and just plain no fun. The easy thing—the natural thing to do is to just let go of the emotions and let them have their way. But that's like unstrapping your safety harness. When emotions rule, chaos and confusion take over.

There's no telling how far you can descend into discouragement, depression, bitterness, anger, resentment, and self-destruction when fleshly emotions rule. The deep end of the emotion pool is a violent, nasty, destructive place for humanity. It's not a place you want to swim.

God gives you an alternative to being ruled by "emotions gone wild." He invites you to "walk in the Spirit." He invites you, like Daniel, to be of an excellent spirit. He extends to you the capacity, through His Spirit, to rule your spirit and to bring your emotions into subjection to truth. And so I challenge you to take the next step.

What do you do when God rewrites your life?

Decision five:

WALK IN THE SPIRIT

Daily yield the control of your emotions and your heart to the power of God's Holy Spirit.

This might sound mystical or spooky, but it's not. It's actually very practical and simple. And it's absolutely life-changing when you're off script.

Emotions lie—a lot. They aren't all bad—after all, God created them. They come in handy in lots of different ways. But fleshly emotions just don't tell the truth. They feed on vain imaginations, fear, and anxiety, and they can lead you to believe things that are absolutely false. If you listen to your emotions you will arrive at a very forlorn and defeated destination—eventually believing God has forsaken you, nobody understands you, and life has just been unfair. You will waste your hardship in the mire of pessimism and self-pity. Your time in darkness will be depressing and self-absorbed. You will mope your way further into despondence through every miserable moment.

Refuse to let emotions call the shots. You have the Spirit of God within you—the potential for a vastly different approach to life's ups and downs. Romans 8:9 calls us to a higher level of living—"But ye are not in the flesh, but in the Spirit, if so be that the Spirit of God dwell in you...."

Speaking of this similar struggle, Romans 6:16 simply tells us it's a choice of yielding—"Know ye not, that to whom ye yield yourselves servants to obey, his servants ye are to whom ye obey; whether of sin unto death, or of obedience unto righteousness?"

If unpredictable events have taken your life in a direction you would not have chosen, you cannot control those events, but you can control your response. By the power of God's Spirit, you can bring emotions into a state of submission and subjection to God's authority. It's a choice. It's an act of the will. It's a decision of obedience. Yield to the Holy Spirit of God and ask Him to control your emotions. Ask Him to give you the mind of Christ. This is when you will find the capacity to genuinely rejoice and hope, even though you are way off script in life.

THANK YOU, LORD, FOR...

In closing this chapter I want to make a difficult suggestion. We've been talking about making good choices—difficult choices—during difficult times. Choosing to rejoice even in a trial—that's a tough choice. Choosing to let God's Spirit control you when powerful emotions are wrestling for control—that's a tough choice. You can make these choices. They are within your reach, by God's enabling.

Let me encourage you to start here with a difficult assignment. Tell God thank you. I know, you think I'm nuts, but just go with me for a moment. This is an exercise in *truth over emotions*. Fact over feelings. God says He wants us to give thanks in everything (1 Thessalonians 5:18). Thankfulness is not an emotion, it's a state of the mind and an act of the will. You can be thankful, whether you feel thankful or not. You can speak thankfulness whether you feel all warm and fuzzy or not. Giving thanks is an act of faith-filled obedience that has nothing to do with your emotions or feelings.

I realize you'd rather feel good about it. You probably equate being thankful with cuddly emotions or warmth. But that's Hollywood. This isn't a Disney movie and you're not a princess. This is real life and in real life *feelings* should be forced to follow *fact*. Truth should rule and emotions will follow.

So, right now, decide to speak thanks, out loud, to your God for your trial. You don't have to be happy about the trial. You don't have to like the trial. You don't have to want another one. You don't have to act like you're enjoying it. Just decide to give thanks. Obey God and say thank you. It will be one of the hardest things you have done, but it will also change you. Try this…

Dear Lord, I love You. I understand that You have ordained this difficult time in my life. I don't like it. I don't understand it. I have a lot of questions. But in spite of all of that... I thank You. Based purely upon the command of Your heart, I follow in obedience, and give thanks. Thank You for... (fill in the blank). Lord, though I don't feel grateful, I proclaim my thanks. I trust Your love, I embrace Your will, I claim Your grace. Thank You, Lord.

I will never forget the first time I said "thank you" for cancer. I pray you will never forget the first time you thank the Lord for your trial. It is an exercise in letting God's Spirit rule emotions. It breaks something in the flesh. It's hard, but it's good to give thanks.

Well, what began as a fairly light-hearted chapter, ended with some real soul searching. I guess that's fitting for a chapter on emotional ups and downs. Perhaps you should spend some time processing all of this.

It's late here and my wife is so thoughtfully holding out my Neupogen injection. I'll see you at the end of the roller coaster ride. And I can promise you, I am not getting back in line—and I'm not buying the photo either!

LIKE A RIVER GLORIOUS

Like a river glorious is God's perfect peace,
Over all victorious, in its bright increase;
Perfect, yet it floweth fuller every day,
Perfect, yet it groweth deeper all the way.

Hidden in the hollow of His blessed hand,
Never foe can follow, never traitor stand;
Not a surge of worry, not a shade of care,
Not a blast of hurry touch the spirit there.

Every joy or trial falleth from above,
Traced upon our dial by the Sun of Love;
We may trust Him fully all for us to do;
They who trust Him wholly find Him wholly true.

—FRANCES R. HAVERGAL

SIX

WAIT AND HOPE IN HIM

*It is of the LORD'S mercies that we are not consumed,
because his compassions fail not. They are new every
morning: great is thy faithfulness.*—LAMENTATIONS 3:22–23

IN SOME WAYS STARTING CHEMO WAS A RELIEF.
For nearly two months I lived with a consuming awareness
that large masses in my chest were expanding and nothing
was being done to stop them. It was a good feeling to finally
know they were shrinking and dying. It was good to be in
"attack mode!"

Amazingly, even before my second treatment I could no
longer feel the swollen lymph nodes under my arm and on
my collar bone. Neither could the doctor. The treatments
appeared to have an immediate effect.

As winter began to settle in, so did the treatment routine.
The Lord allowed the timing of treatments to fall in a way
that we still enjoyed a twenty-first wedding anniversary and

Christmas as a family. But shortly after, treatment three seemed to take the trial to another level. The doctor had warned me that the chemo would have a cumulative impact, so I expected things to get worse. And they did.

Chemotherapy kills rapidly reproducing cells—of all sorts. It impacts the good cells as well as the bad ones. For cancer cells that's good. But for white blood cells (the immune system), the digestive system, and other areas of your body like the inside of your mouth, that's bad. As far as my particular chemo, I read stories on both ends of the spectrum. Some people were sick for only a few days, while others were wiped out perpetually through treatment. I would have to wait and see how my body would respond.

The nausea was manageable with medications most of the time. But along with nausea, the chemo sort of shuts the body down. It sends the physical functions into a shocked state of alarm in dealing with chemicals it has never processed before. People say, "flu-like" symptoms, but that falls way short. This is no flu.

At the worst peak moments of treatment, all I could do was crawl into bed and endure. The brain just seems to shut down and not be able to think. About the most it wants to do is watch *I Love Lucy* re-runs or news programs. Headaches were intense and frequent, aches and pains were varied, appetite would come and go, though most food had no taste for several days.

It's a guessing game as to what kind of food your digestive system can handle in any given moment, and every few hours there are five or six more pills to take to manage all the impacts of the chemo. It would take me a whole chapter to list and describe each one and their function. Suffice to say, I have one of those compartmentalized pill cases that elderly people carry, one for each day, and each compartment is just about overflowing every day. My cupboard looks like a pharmacy.

WELCOME TO CHEMO-CAVE

Along with the chemo, the nurses administer a steroid designed to help the body respond better to the chemo, but not in a way that you feel. The steroid brought its own problems—like racing brain, that inability to sleep well because mundane thoughts are racing all night through your mind, like making your bed. And so rather than sleeping, you toss and turn all night while your brain finds a million and one ways to make and remake your bed. You wake up exhausted, but with a lot of fresh bed-making ideas.

Day to day, night to night there was nothing to do but endure—just waiting for God to get me through. I call it the "chemo-cave"—it's a dark, horrible place where your brain and body go during the most intense moments of treatments. You can't think or respond much. You can't relate or converse.

You just withdraw and use whatever cognitive abilities you have to hang in there and wait—and maybe moan a little. (Somebody please tell me, *why does that help?*)

For Haylee, my daughter, I came up with a little nickname for the chemo-cave days. We called me *Sickme*. I would pray with Haylee the night before treatment and say, "*Sickme* will be back for a few days. He loves you very much, he just can't show it very well, so be nice to him, and I'll see you on the other side. Tell *Sickme* I don't like him!" She would smile, pat my head, and say, "I love *Sickme*."

And after several days in chemo-cave, as the chemical effects start to diminish, the brain emerges first. Mental clarity returns before physical abilities. Then over the next few days, the body starts to come out as well.

The third, fourth, and fifth treatments became increasingly harder. My body grew gradually weaker and wasn't recovering as well during the two week breaks. The lack of white blood cells also created a massive lack of energy and physical strength—along with a case of bronchitis that hung on for a few weeks. Just getting dressed in the morning would take the wind out of me. If I walked up stairs, I would have to sit down for a moment to regain strength. And the three flights of stairs up to my church office really set me back.

These experiences were bizarre for a guy that usually takes two or three steps at a time and lives with a seemingly endless supply of energy. Suddenly I felt like I was eighty years old. Now my energy supply seemed very limited and directly impacted by what I ate within the last hour. I was functioning constantly on a very low fuel guage, and almost always drinking or nibbling on something, just to find a little energy.

Two of the most depleting exercises were teaching God's Word or leading in church services. Thankfully, through most of my treatments, I've been able to be in church most of the time. But I never realized how much energy it takes to teach a lesson or lead a service. There's nothing I love more than teaching the Word of God, so I have jumped at every opportunity to do so, even while sick. But those moments take everything out of me and usually leave me feeling weak and sickly for a day or more.

One of the more comical sides of chemo has been what is called "chemo-brain." Basically, these chemicals are killing brain cells, whether we want them to or not. And with every additional treatment, I get a little larger case of chemo-brain. It's extremely entertaining to my family—especially to Dana, who in my opinion, has had chemo-brain as long as I've known her. I tease her that God gave me chemo because I have enough brain-cells to spare. But she's had the upper hand mentally for the last few months. She's really enjoying it!

Over the past months I've forgotten basic things, struggled to find the words I'm trying to say, and generally acted a bit spaced-out and disconnected at times. My wife loves it because she enjoys laughing at me. For her it's sweet revenge after I've laughed at her so much over the years. My kids pretty much laugh too. And when they do, I just put on an incredulous and victimized look and say, "Oh, sure. Here I am dying of cancer. Laugh it up! In my condition! Sure, just have a good time!" They know I'm kidding, and they've gotten use to me joking around and milking this experience for everything it's worth.

The good side of chemo is that my family has to get me anything I need or want as soon as I ask for it. It's a sort of unspoken law of the chemotherapy experience. So our house is filled with the consistent flow of requests from the pathetic chemo patient: "Larry, can you bring me a chocolate milk?" "Dana, can you go get me a breakfast burrito from that café?" "Haylee, since I'm sick, can you tickle my back?" "Lance, since I have cancer, can you wash my car and put gas in it?" Generally they respond with a good spirit, except when they know I'm feeling fine. Then they look at me like, *your taking this a bit too far.*

I have a feeling there's some serious payback coming when I'm healthy again. I'm definitely spoiled right now, and I've got to be honest—part of me is loving it!

PATIENTLY ENDURING

Off script times, especially those that involve suffering, require *endurance*. This isn't something you will find within yourself, especially if you're as big of a wimp as I am—medically speaking. If you try to look within yourself for strength, patience, and the ability to endure, you'll likely go insane. Humanly speaking, these times are just nuts! It's impossible to wrap your brain around all that's happening, much less what it means and where it's headed.

God doesn't intend your trial to take you to the brink of sanity. He intends it to bring you into His presence, and thus His strength. He speaks of this in Hebrews 6—a book written specifically to help new Christians to mature in God's strength and grace. In chapter 6 the Lord is challenging the Christians to move forward in their faith, in full assurance of hope until the end. He reminds the reader of those who patiently hoped and waited through trials until they obtained God's promises. He uses Abraham as the key example. Look at what God says in verse 15:

> And so, *after he had patiently endured, he obtained the promise.*—HEBREWS 6:15

"*Patiently endured*" are the words God uses. He speaks of this again in Hebrews 10 in reminding the believers that they were saved and immediately entered into a *"great fight of afflictions."* Then God challenges us:

> Cast not away therefore your confidence, which hath
> great recompence of reward. For ye have need of
> patience, that, after ye have done the will of God, ye
> might receive the promise. —HEBREWS 10:35–36

God says we have need of patience. Don't cast away your confidence during this great fight of afflictions. Don't lose hope. Don't stop believing that God is good and that God keeps His promises. He promises us that the enduring, the patient suffering will not last forever. There will come a moment when you have accomplished the will of God and will receive the promise. This is all going somewhere, and it's all too important for you to lose faith or hope. Hear the voice of God through His Word essentially saying, "Hang in there! I'm going to make it worth it!"

Worth it!

That's what this trial will one day be in your memory—worth it! That's what the words *great recompence of reward* mean. *Great*—huge, massive, enormous. *Recompence*—repayment, pay-back, an earned wage. *Reward*—the treasures of darkness and hidden riches of secret places, the riches of the grace and goodness of God.

Yes, one day, if you patiently endure, you will look back on this off script, dark time and think, *That was worth it!*

You may not see it or feel it now, but God's promise is more certain than the sunrise! It will happen, if you finish this course—if you refuse to cast off your confidence.

WAIT AND HOPE IN HIM

Have you ever been in an earthquake? Living in Southern California, we've experienced our fair share of them. People do funny things during earthquakes. People do unreasonable things—things that make no sense at all to human rationale. The first thing they do is freeze in panic. Everything that was once stable and solid is suddenly shaking. That can instantly bring the human mind to frozen fear. When the whole world is shaking, it sort of rattles you to the core.

The next thing they do is run. Literally, they find an open place and start running—as though they can run from the shaking and find another place of stability down the road somewhere. It makes no sense. When the whole world is shaking, where can you run? What possible good could running do? Strange creatures we are.

The premeditated response—the well-trained response is to maintain your whits and quickly find a table to hide under or a door jamb to stand in until the shaking passes. In a serious earthquake, your worst chances of survival are in panicking or in running down the street. Your greatest chances of survival are found in hiding yourself in the most stable close-by place and waiting for the earthquake to end.

How we hate to wait, especially in off script places. In trials we want to do the same thing that many people do in earthquakes. We either freeze in panic and fear, or we start running and taking matters into our own hands. Either way, we start to scramble for options, frantically searching for solutions, survival, stability. We want the world to stop shaking as soon as possible. We want our script back right away. But that's often not how God is leading.

God wants the shaking of your world to loosen your grip on the reins of your life. He providentially leads us into hardship bigger than we could possibly control. He ordains and allows circumstances against which we are absolutely and utterly powerless. No amount of human anxiety, anguish, or exertion will make a difference. In these places, we are altogether powerless. No solution lies within our grasp. No escape beckons our attention.

Helpless—but not hopeless.

God may lead you to a place where you are helpless in your own strength, but never to a place where you are without help. You may feel hopeless in your own power, but you are never without hope. What is it that God wants us to do in these seemingly helpless and hopeless places? This is what Jeremiah learned—and teaches us.

Lamentations 3 is awesome. In fact, God's whole Word is awesome! The life of Jeremiah is an amazing story. God called him as a young man to be a preacher. You can read the story in Jeremiah.

In chapter 1, God calls Jeremiah, he panics but surrenders, and then God tells him it's not going to be easy. And it wasn't. Jeremiah had a very difficult road, but God promised Jeremiah that He would be with him and that the trials he would suffer would not overtake him. Essentially, God said, "Jeremiah, you're going to suffer some, but I'm going to be with you through it all, and you win in the end, so stick with me and don't lose hope!"

Well, Lamentations 3 finds Jeremiah in a very low moment, very transparent and frankly, a bit raw. It's a hard chapter to read, and even harder to process—and it happened to be the chapter that the Lord led me to the night before my first chemo treatment. Amazing. It was exactly what I needed. Maybe it will help you too. Let's read the hard stuff first:

> *I am the man that hath seen affliction by the rod of his wrath. He hath led me, and brought me into darkness, but not into light. Surely against me is he turned; he turneth his hand against me all the day. My flesh and my skin hath he made old; he hath broken my bones. He hath builded against me, and compassed me with gall and travail. He hath set me in dark places, as they that*

be dead of old. He hath hedged me about, that I cannot get out: he hath made my chain heavy. Also when I cry and shout, he shutteth out my prayer. He hath inclosed my ways with hewn stone, he hath made my paths crooked. He was unto me as a bear lying in wait, and as a lion in secret places. He hath turned aside my ways, and pulled me in pieces: he hath made me desolate. He hath bent his bow, and set me as a mark for the arrow. He hath caused the arrows of his quiver to enter into my reins. I was a derision to all my people; and their song all the day. He hath filled me with bitterness, he hath made me drunken with wormwood. He hath also broken my teeth with gravel stones, he hath covered me with ashes. And thou hast removed my soul far off from peace: I forgat prosperity. And I said, My strength and my hope is perished from the LORD: Remembering mine affliction and my misery, the wormwood and the gall. My soul hath them still in remembrance, and is humbled in me.—LAMENTATIONS 3:1–20

Sounds like a man totally forsaken by God, doesn't it? Sounds flat scary! When I read this chapter I thought, *it shouldn't be called chemo, it should be called wormwood—and yes, God is about to fill me with bitterness and make me drunken with wormwood.*

In this chapter, Jeremiah is a man pouring out to God his raw human pain and emotions. He even voiced his complaints and disappointments with God. Isn't it amazing that God not only listened to the cries of his heart, but He recorded them for us! Sounds to me as if God wants to hear exactly how you feel—and since He already knows, you can't really hide it from Him any way.

Perhaps you can identify with the pain and transparent emotions of Jeremiah. I would encourage you to follow his example—to cast all of your care upon God, knowing that He cares for you, no matter how raw or brutal your prayer may sound. God already knows. When you do this, something special will happen. Let's continue to read:

> *This I recall to my mind, therefore have I hope. It is of the LORD'S mercies that we are not consumed, because his compassions fail not. They are new every morning: great is thy faithfulness. The LORD is my portion, saith my soul; therefore will I hope in him. The LORD is good unto them that wait for him, to the soul that seeketh him. It is good that a man should both hope and quietly wait for the salvation of the LORD.*
> —LAMENTATIONS 3:21–26

God met Jeremiah in the middle of his emotional meltdown, and reminded him of a few things. God brought some new perspective to Jeremiah's mind. Compassion, mercy, faithfulness, hope! Like a fresh well-spring of water on a parched soul, these verses burst directly onto the page of the darkest day in Jeremiah's life—and yours and mine. *The LORD is good unto them that wait for him. It is good that a man should both hope and quietly wait for the salvation of the LORD.* Wow!

What do you do when God rewrites the script of your life?

Decision six:
WAIT ON GOD AND HOPE IN HIM

Decide to patiently endure the circumstances He has ordained, and wait with hope in Him!

THE SUFFICIENCY OF GRACE

There are times in life when all you can do is *wait* and *hope*. All you can do is get through it with God and His grace. And while waiting and hoping feels like you're doing nothing, you are actually doing the *most important* thing you can do! You may be powerless to change the circumstances or fix the problem, but you are not powerless to respond. Your life may be off script, but it is not headed nowhere. You may *feel* like your life is paused and pointless, but nothing could be farther from the truth. *Waiting and hoping in God are sometimes the two most productive and purposeful things you can do!*

The Christian life is one of obeying God. And if God has led you into a hard place of suffering, your mission from Him is to patiently wait and hope in Him. Endure the hardship with your heart fixed upon Him, and hope to the end. Know that He is working. Know that His promises will be fulfilled.

Jeremiah continues a few verses later:

> *For the Lord will not cast off for ever: But though he cause grief, yet will he have compassion according to the multitude of his mercies. For he doth not afflict willingly nor grieve the children of men.*
> —LAMENTATIONS 3:31–33

God isn't flippant about putting you through hardness. He doesn't derive any personal pleasure in seeing you suffer. The exact opposite is true. During your suffering, He desires to pour out His compassionate mercies, to strengthen your heart, and to sustain you through the storm.

I haven't suffered much. In all honesty, though cancer and chemo are terrible experiences, I know many people who have suffered far beyond my meager months of illness. I'm no pro at suffering, but I have learned something in this valley. When God says in 2 Corinthians 12:9, "...My grace is sufficient for thee: for my strength is made perfect in weakness..." it's true.

God doesn't call you to endure or wait or hope in your own strength. He intends to supply His grace to enable you to do the job. And His grace is a daily, moment-by-moment portion. You will have the grace you need, when you need it—not a moment sooner and not a moment later.

From the outside looking in, that doesn't make sense. But it's an up-close reality in the trial. If you had asked me before cancer how I would cope with having cancer, I would have been unable to answer. I would have had no idea how to respond. But in every moment of every day—even in the chemo-cave—God meets me there with just enough of His grace to get me through.

With every chemo infusion, there is apparently a *grace infusion*. Because in my opinion, I should have lost my mind a long time ago. God's grace keeps patience and hope alive. God's grace enables patient endurance. God's grace is a very real-time, dynamic sufficiency. You will experience it when you need it—so long as you are waiting and hoping in Him.

God's grace can cause you to take the attitude of the rest of the verse we just saw: "...Most gladly therefore will I rather glory in my infirmities, that the power of Christ may rest upon me" (2 Corinthians 12:9). Paul said, "Hey, it's not fun, but it's worth it and God's grace makes it doable!

BE IT UNTO ME

It may not be Christmas, but go with me to the Christmas story for a moment. Do you ever find yourself connecting in different ways with characters in the Christmas story? Have you ever seen yourself in the worshipping shepherds, the seeking wise men, or the waiting Simeon? I suppose we all find varying connection points with the many players in this cast.

This past Christmas, for me, was quite different. I found my heart resonating with Mary. Not her youth (I wish!). Not her gender (no matter what my health care provider thinks!). Not her child bearing (thank you, Lord!). No, I connected with the fact that she received startling news that essentially rewrote the script of her life. In a moment, all of her expectations were upended—like a rug pulled out from under her. Whatever her plans were, everything changed with one word from an Angelic messenger.

Like you, I've heard the story a million times, but I was eager to learn from Mary once again—this time at a whole new level. She was resolute. Calm. At peace. Ready to be and do whatever God chose. When she could have been fearful—she was steady. When she should have been nervous, anxious, and worried—she was steadfast and patient. When she might have been resistant, hesitant, or reticent—she was unquestioningly confident. Poised. She was assured and secure.

Why? How? She's just been given very bitter-sweet news—sweet in that this was Messiah and she was chosen. Bitter in that, who would really believe her story? Undoubtedly, she was entering a life that would forever be haunted by gossip, shadowed by disbelief, and trailed by public dismissal and hushed whispers. How could she respond with such strength and faith?

She truly was surrendered. She knew the meaning of the title "Lord." She recognized who she was in God's plan—His handmaid—a female servant. And she chose to rejoice—to delight abundantly in God's plan.

In our off script moments may we long in our hearts to emulate Mary's heart—to be like her in the depth of her love and submission to God and the abundance of her rejoicing and delight in His plan. Think of her words in Luke 1:38—"…Behold the handmaid of the Lord; be it unto me according to thy word…." Again, in Luke 1:46-47—"My soul doth magnify the Lord, And my spirit hath rejoiced in God my Saviour…."

Waiting, hoping, patiently enduring whatever God has ordained. It's all in His hands, and I am His servant.

When I replay how the script of my life has changed so dramatically, I consider Mary's response: "Be it unto me according to thy Word. Behold the handmaid of the Lord."

Wow. I want to have that heart. "God I am your servant. Do with me whatever you choose."

When I look into the uncertainty of the future, perhaps like you, I stare into the face of questions: the months of treatments, the potential for healing and remission, the possibilities of recurrence, the eventual possibilities of further treatments or even stem cell transplant, and the long-term risks of other forms of cancer or risks related to treatment. I recognize that God has providentially allowed my life to turn a direction I would never have chosen.

Mary made the right decision. To glorify the Lord—to wait, hope, and patiently endure that she might receive His promise.

So, here we are—off script. There's nothing we can do to "fix" it because it isn't broken. There's nothing we can do to change it, because God has taken our hands off the reigns. Powerless. Humanly helpless. Absolutely and utterly inadequate to the challenge, we stand in complete and total vulnerability.

Be patient. Wait upon the Lord. Hope in Him. For if you refuse to cast off your confidence, one day, you will look back on this very moment and say two words.

"Worth it!"

The Solid Rock

My hope is built on nothing less
Than Jesus' blood and righteousness;
I dare not trust the sweetest frame,
But wholly lean on Jesus' name.

When darkness veils His lovely face,
I rest on His unchanging grace;
In every high and stormy gale,
My anchor holds within the veil.

His oath, His covenant, His blood
Support me in the whelming flood;
When all around my soul gives way,
He then is all my hope and stay.

When He shall come with trumpet sound,
Oh, may I then in Him be found;
Dressed in His righteousness alone,
Faultless to stand before the throne.

On Christ, the solid Rock, I stand;
All other ground is sinking sand,
All other ground is sinking sand.

—Edward Mote

SEVEN
TRY YOUR WAYS

Knowing this, that the trying of your faith worketh patience.
But let patience have her perfect work, that ye may
be perfect and entire, wanting nothing.—JAMES 1:3–4

"OOPS... I'M SO SORRY..." THIS HAS BECOME MY opening line more than I care to admit. The scene, on a sick day, is something like this. I'm convalescing in some reclined position, propped up by pillows in bed or on the couch, without much strength.

It's mid-morning. Dana has awakened long before me, helped the kids start their day, worked around the house, and done her absolute best to keep our room quiet so I can sleep. Her favorite trick is to surround me with little electric fans so their humming will mask out the sound of the kids preparing for school. It works, but when I actually do wake up I generally feel like I'm sleeping in a manufacturing plant for small electric fans or toy airplanes.

Back to the scene. So, I've managed to prop myself up and begin needing. I need water. Gatorade. An orange. A pop-tart. Oatmeal. Saltine crackers. Pills. More pills. Help. On the list could go—completely random and extremely urgent. Like, I need this... ten minutes ago!

On three separate occasions my wonderful wife brings me a drink—in this case chocolate milk. (For some reason chocolate settles my stomach on sick days.) She hands it to me, walks away, and crash—I spill it. I don't mean I bump a little out onto the carpet or bed. I don't mean I drip a little onto my shirt. I mean complete and utter motor-skill failure—the whole glass is dumped upside down onto something costly. Once on the carpet. Once on the couch. And once on her favorite pillow shams.

This is where the "Oops... I'm so sorry..." line comes in. All three times, she stops, turns and I do my best to put on a "poor-puppy-dog look"—as milk drips and flows all around me. Then she laughs. She's not laughing at me—like ridicule. She's laughing with me—like "I'm raising a three year old again!" The last time she said, "I'm buying you some sippy cups!" And we both laughed.

We decided from now on she will bring me two glasses. The first one I will just dump out all around me, the second one I will drink from.

The good news is, I have an awesome excuse for random muscular anomalies that cause drink glasses to dump onto the nearest permanent fixture—"side effects."

This story is a microcosm of our recent home-life—our somewhat humorous adventure with cancer and all its related experiences and side-effects. Not only does my brain not work and my body become dysfunctional—I'm losing motor-skills and abilities of coordination. And honestly, through all this, Dana has become my "hero" in life. She has quite literally become, to me, a living portrait of God's grace and mercy— His unmerited favor, and withheld punishment. Her care, patience, and sacrifice have been indescribable.

During this trial, Dana has made our home a haven in every sense of the word. Every waking moment she's anticipating needs, planning care, providing medication, handling phone calls to and from doctors, cleaning up messes, fulfilling odd meal requests, and doing anything in her power to make my life with chemo more tolerable. Never have I felt like such a burden to others—especially her. It seems I say, "I'm so sorry" about one hundred times a day, but her response is nothing less than eager love! All of this in addition to the regular running of a busy household with three kids who generate a lot of laundry and appetites!

She sits with me while I'm having treatments. She stands behind me supportively "cringing" while I'm giving myself an injection. She wakes up before me so she can be ready to help. She stays up later to do the things she couldn't get done during the day. And from morning to evening she expends herself for those she loves.

On more than a few occasions my heart has ached for my wife and kids through this. What's it like to have a spouse or a dad dealing with cancer? Big bummer, I'm sure. But with Dana, you honestly wouldn't know it. To know her, to be married to her, and to have her love and care certainly makes me one of the most blessed people in the world!

BIG QUESTIONS FOR A BIG GOD

Isn't that like our relationship with God? We are indescribably undeserving and helpless—even pathetic. He is indescribably good and gracious—unbelievably merciful. He knows the worst about us, and loves us no less. He is acquainted with every complaint and discontentment, and blesses us without end. We are but dust, yet He bestows us with value. We are worms, but He redeems us as His own. We are sinful beings, but He adopts us as children.

We bring Him nothing but a mess, and He cleans it up in love.

We are destitute beings with absolutely nothing to offer Him, yet He offers us all that He is. How could we resist such a God? How could we run from such a Father? How could we question such a heart?

So often, in trials, we wrestle with big questions about God. Our unfounded expectation of a life of ease has misled our hearts. Our unwise belief that God owes us a good life leads us to question His nature and heart when life goes off script and becomes unpleasant. Rather than consider all the messes we've made in life and God's great grace in cleaning us up by His redeeming love, we descend into unfounded and unfair assault.

Why me? What does God think He's doing? Is God mad at me? Is God punishing me? What did I do to deserve this? Did I make God angry? Why does God allow bad things to happen to good people?

God isn't an angry old man running an orphanage. His ways in no way resemble our human ways of crime and punishment, violation and justice, or offense and vengeance. To be sure, God is just. To be sure, sin requires punishment— or payment. To be sure, God is not soft on sin and there is a coming final judgment or vengeance on all sin. But if you are His child, you have a completely different relationship with Him.

Let's be honest, in many ways we could turn the questions around. Why not me? Why not more suffering? Knowing I'm sinful, why would God bless me at all? Why does a good God allow good things to happen to bad people? Why has God been so good to me when I know how undeserving I am?

Is God Punishing Me?

Still, we wrestle with the concept of what God is doing in our hard times. Is He punishing us? Is He angry with us? The simple and absolute answer is *no*. God is not punishing you, and He isn't angry with you. Now, those are big claims, so let me back them up with principle and Scripture.

First, the Bible does portray the wrath and anger of God, even at times with His chosen people Israel. But in relation to His redeemed children—those covered in the blood of Christ on the Cross—God never refers or relates to them in Scripture in anger. God does not deal with you or me in anger, nor does He punish us in the sense that we think of punishment. Why? How could this be true? Quite simply— the Cross!

If you have trusted Christ's payment on the Cross for your sin, then I have good news for you. All the wrath of God, all the anger of God, all the righteous judgment of God, and all the punishment of God for sin—including yours—was poured out upon Jesus on the Cross. There's nothing left to punish. There's nothing left to be angry about. It is finished! It is paid in full—absolute, complete, nothing left to be done.

Punishment is *punitive*. It is of *retribution* and *atonement*. In human terms, in parenting terms, we might think that doing wrong brings punishment. When you lied to your parents, you were grounded, and that was your punishment. We fling that word around without considering its meaning. And the problem in our human relationships is that we don't think like God. We focus more on punishment—the payment for the crime—and we leave out the chastening and the nurture, or the learning and teaching aspects of recovering and growing from wrong. We make sure the crime is paid for, but we don't help the child or offender grow to become a different person.

In your relationship with God, He dealt all the punishment and fulfilled His righteous and just demands for sin through the death of Jesus on the Cross. If you have accepted that payment, then you have no sin left for which to pay, no crimes left for which to atone, no offenses to your record that require retribution.

As 1 John 2 states, when you sin, you have an advocate with the Father, Jesus Christ the righteous, who stands on your behalf as the full payment for sin. It is Jesus' death that prevents God from needing to punish you or deal with you in anger. There's no anger left. There's no punishment left.

And if there is—then the Cross wasn't enough. Jesus didn't really pay it all.

So, no—God is not angry with you. God is not punishing you. God is not your terrible task-master, your angry school principal, or your harsh parent demanding that you take your punishment for whatever you have done. Your trial is not punishment. Put that thought away forever! Don't ever let Satan falsely accuse God in your heart.

Quick — Run and Hide

Before we discover what God is doing, let's dig a little deeper into this topic.

When you were growing up and you did something wrong, what did you fear? Probably being caught and being punished. Most kids are just hoping to stay out of trouble. They don't want to be punished.

So, what did you do when you did something wrong? You hid it. You covered your tracks. You did whatever you needed to do to avoid punishment.

And when you got caught, what did you do? You lied. You blamed something or someone else. You rationalized. You excused yourself. You may have even run and hid. You became good at covering your sin, and when it was uncovered, you became good at doing anything you could to avoid blame and punishment. It all boiled down to the punishment. You really, really didn't want to get spanked, grounded, or yelled at.

And all too often we bring these practices and human rationale into our relationship with God. We see God as we saw human authority (parents, teachers, etc.) and we carry over our earthly behavior into the spiritual relationship with our Heavenly Father—all because we don't understand the nature of this relationship, or we forget it.

As children of God, we fail. We sin. And when we do, we tend to cover it. We pretend it isn't there. We sort of lie to God, blame-shift, rationalize it away, or run from God. But all the while, it's remaining unacknowledged and unconfessed in our day-to-day relationship with God. Why do we do this? To avoid punishment. It's the same game. We think God is going to smack us, so we run and hide.

Let me be plain. God doesn't want you to view your relationship with Him in this light, and He's gone to great lengths to make a different kind of relationship possible. He doesn't want you dealing with sin in this way. So let's rethink this.

First, the sin problem is already paid for and dealt with through Christ at the Cross. The punishment for everything you will ever do wrong is already dealt and paid! There's nothing left to pay. God has removed the need for you to run and hide. He has completely abolished any need or motivation you may have to cover your sin or lie to Him. He doesn't stand with a belt in his hand demanding that you "bend over!" You have nothing to gain with God by playing this game because He isn't planning to punish you.

It's the exact opposite. He stands with arms open, like the father of the prodigal, inviting you to come back to Him. He invites you, in Isaiah 1, "Come now, and let us reason together, though your sins be as scarlet, they shall be as white as snow…." He has dealt with your sin, and His simple requirement in 1 John 1 is that you *confess it*. He desires that you *acknowledge* your sin, not pay for it. He wants you to *forsake* your sin, not hide it. His justice is satisfied, so the only thing left to do is keep the relationship clean by confessing and acknowledging sin.

I'M SO SORRY

If in the midst of your trial, you find yourself with chocolate milk spilled all over the place, you have been given a golden opportunity by God to step back and "try your ways"—to allow the hardship to bring about life change, personal growth, and Holy Spirit-led course-correction. And when that examination exposes sin that perhaps you weren't even aware of, you can accept God's invitation to deal with that sin by His grace and unconditional love. He simply asks that you acknowledge and confess, and He promises to forgive you and cleanse you from all unrighteousness. He promises to clean up the mess. Look at it for yourself:

> *If we say that we have no sin, we deceive ourselves, and the truth is not in us. If we confess our sins, he is faithful and just to forgive us our sins, and to cleanse us from all unrighteousness.*—1 JOHN 1:8–9

Those verses do not demand retribution. They invite confession and restoration. They say, "stop playing the game, and start being honest with yourself and with God." How this could dramatically change our relationship with our Heavenly Father!

Every time you sin, your Heavenly Father waits for you, not to pay for the sin but to confess it. And when you do, your relationship with Him is renewed in closeness and intimacy. No payment required—that's what the Cross was for. What amazing love!

Now, I realize you're probably thinking—what am I missing here? I know God doesn't just put up with our sin. You are correct. He doesn't. First, if you haven't gotten this already—it isn't punishment. It isn't punitive or payment related. Second, remember this—God invites you, on the other side of every single sin, to simply come back to Him. Of your own free will, confess. Acknowledge the sin and return to God. This door is always open, and you can never confess or acknowledge sin too many times. All of your sin has been paid.

Simply put, the problem isn't that our sin needs to be paid for—it needs to be purged. Even as children of God, we can love our sin and hold onto it. We can allow it to remain in our lives, separating us relationally from the Lord, but damaging our hearts and lives. And sometimes we can even be blind to it. God loves us too much, as His children, to allow this to continue. While He doesn't require payment, He also won't ignore our sin or our need for growth. He intervenes.

So, What Is God Really Up To?

This chapter is not designed to be an exhaustive treatment of all types of suffering or hardship, but in general, there are several potential types of negative circumstances in life:

First—the anger and judgment of God upon sin. We've already ruled that one out for the child of God.

Second—the natural consequences of sin. These are the built in bad things that happen in life as a natural result of sin. This isn't judgment or anger, it's just the simple outcome of doing wrong. If I stick my finger into a light socket, the resulting electrocution isn't the judgment of God, it's just the result of being dumb.

Third—spiritual warfare or sifting. Many times in Scripture we find the enemy resisting God's children. All of these times are "Father-filtered" but they are legitimate times of hardship nonetheless.

Fourth—a trial allowed by God uniquely for His glory. Job is a good example of this. God allowed Job's hardship for the high calling and purpose of glorifying Himself.

Fifth—the chastening of our loving Father. This is when God intervenes to bring correction and growth in my life through pain, and His intent is to purge sin from my life and take me forward in fruitfulness for His greater glory. *Chastening* is the focus of this chapter.

Chastening is not God's *fury*—it is His *favor*!

Chasten—this is a great word. It doesn't mean punishment. It doesn't mean payment. It means "to discipline, nurture, teach, or train." While God doesn't punish His children, He does *chasten* them. He does desire to teach, train, nurture, and discipline. He will most certainly correct us.

Before you get ahead of me—there is no way for me to know what specific aspects of your trial are God's chastening or correction in your life. That's between you and God to discover. But I can't imagine experiencing any hardship in this life without asking God to use it as a purging and growing experience to make me more like Christ and to bring greater glory to Him in the process.

While *punishment* is merely concerned with restitution and justice, *chastening* has no such concerns. Chastening is future focused and always looks upward in hope toward an expected outcome for the good. Chastening is driven by love and tender compassion, and is designed to keep me growing in the right direction spiritually. Chastening is designed to bring forth the peaceable fruit of righteousness in your life and future.

Hebrews 12 teaches us much of this word. Let's read and then examine:

6 For whom the Lord loveth he chasteneth, and scourgeth every son whom he receiveth. 7 If ye endure chastening, God dealeth with you as with sons; for what son is he whom the father chasteneth not? 8 But if ye be without chastisement, whereof all are partakers, then are ye bastards, and not sons. 9 Furthermore we have had fathers of our flesh which corrected us, and we gave them reverence: shall we not much rather be in subjection unto the Father of spirits, and live? 10 For they verily for a few days chastened us after their own pleasure; but he for our profit, that we might be partakers of his holiness. 11 Now no chastening for the present seemeth to be joyous, but grievous: nevertheless afterward it yieldeth the peaceable fruit of righteousness unto them which are exercised thereby. 12 Wherefore lift up the hands which hang down, and the feeble knees; 13 And make straight paths for your feet, lest that which is lame be turned out of the way; but let it rather be healed. 14 Follow peace with all men, and holiness, without which no man shall see the Lord: 15 Looking diligently lest any man fail of the grace of God; lest any root of bitterness springing up trouble you, and thereby many be defiled;
—HEBREWS 12:6–15

While not all Christian suffering could be quantified as *chastening*, let's consider this important passage for a moment. We see in verses 6 and 11 that chastening is painful. We see though, in verses 8–10, that it's completely different than earthly parenting. God deals with us as His children, and His chastening is always for our profit—never His pleasure. We see in verse 11 that chastening from God always has an "afterward" that bears new fruit in our lives. Through chastening we mature, we grow, and we emerge more like Christ.

In verses 12–15 God gives us a pattern for responding to chastening. It includes making peace in our relationships, adjusting our attitude toward it, refusing to become bitter, and claiming grace to get through the chastening in a way that makes us better not bitter. And we see the warning of failing the grace of God and allowing bitterness to spring up, trouble us, and defile us and others.

This is a quick summary, so I encourage you to dive into this passage on your own. It is rich with truth and application. The big take away is simply this:

In the hardship, take time to consider the fact that God may be purging you, purifying you, preparing you. He may be pruning your life in the winter so that you might bring forth greater fruit in the summer. It's painful, but it's not punishment. Doesn't that make a huge difference? I doubt that I could bear my trial if I believed God were punishing me. But knowing He is chastening me makes it more than bearable—it makes it hopeful!

The principle of chastening energizes the whole process with anticipation and almost *intrigue!* What is God going to grow out of all of this pain and hardship? I almost can't wait to see! It gives the off script time an eager awaiting—a sense of someday, somehow, someway—this is all working something very, very good! That's God. That's who He is. That's what He does!

Don't you just LOVE Him? Wow—what a Father!

TRY YOUR WAYS

Too often, our response to hardship is to complain. But in light of the things we've seen in this chapter—there's really nothing to complain about. God is all good, and we have nothing to offer Him but a mess. So, in the hardship, the right response is to patiently accept the chastening work of God, and to let that work have its way in our hearts and lives. It's like laying down on the surgeon's table and saying, "Okay, Lord, do what you need to do in me." We have nothing but flaws and weakness to lose, and everything in the character of Christ to gain. And God promises that we will emerge more mature—more perfect in Christ.

> My brethren, count it all joy when ye fall into divers temptations; Knowing this, that the trying of your faith worketh patience. But let patience have her perfect

that ye may be perfect and entire, wanting nothing.
—JAMES 1:2–4

Back in Lamentations 3, there's a verse we didn't look at. Remember all the hardship and raw emotion of the chapter? But toward the end, Jeremiah says this in verses 39–41:

Wherefore doth a living man complain, a man for the punishment of his sins? Let us search and try our ways, and turn again to the LORD. Let us lift up our heart with our hands unto God in the heavens.

Complain? What right have we to complain in the light of what we deserve? Rather let us respond differently. And this is the point of this whole chapter. All the study of punishment and sin and redemption leads to this response.

What do you do when God rewrites your life?

Decision seven:
TRY YOUR WAYS

Let God search your heart and let this God-allowed trial purge and shape you into the image of Jesus Christ.

It's not about beating ourselves up over our past. It's not about descending into remorse. It's about letting the present pain produce perfection—maturity in Christ. It's about allowing the trial to cause us to step back and "try our ways"—to change our lives for the better.

An off script season should be a *refining time*. It should cause us to allow the Holy Spirit of God to once again "Search me, O God, and know my heart: try me, and know my thoughts: And see if there be any wicked way in me, and lead me in the way everlasting" (Psalms 139:23-4).

Hardship should compel us to pause and examine our lives. Through the fiery trial, our desire should be to "come forth as gold" (Job 23:10). Whether your life was off track spiritually before your trial or not, don't miss this opportunity to allow God to refine and purge areas of your life of which you weren't even aware.

Should you descend into doubts and despair over whether God is punishing you? Absolutely not. Should you allow God to search your heart for anything He desires to purge and prune away in winter so that more fruit can be born in summer? Absolutely.

A living man—especially a saved man, certainly has no right to complain before the Lord. How blessed we are that God doesn't deal with us according to our sin and His justice. If all God ever did was save me—giving the life of Christ for my ransom, then any burden He allows in this life should pale in comparison to salvation. In light of salvation, whatever God chooses to do with the rest of my life should be just fine!

Simply put, the right response to affliction is to examine ourselves, draw close to God, be purged by His hand, and allow patience to have her perfect work in our hearts and through our lives.

Matthew Henry said it this way: "Happy shall we be, if we learn to receive affliction as laid upon us by the hand of God... While there is life there is hope; and instead of complaining that things are bad, we should encourage ourselves with the hope they will be better. We are sinful men, and what we complain of, is far less than our sins deserve. We should complain to God, and not of him."

I love that! "What we complain of is far less than our sins deserve." How true! And then the challenge—complain to God, not of Him! As much as God hates murmuring (complaining from a bitter spirit against His heart), He welcomes mourning (bringing our truthful hearts, mournful communications, and our very burden to Him)! He throws open the throne room of Heaven and invites us—fallen, pathetic creatures—to boldly cast all of our cares upon Him and to find grace to help in time of need. He doesn't expect us to relish the afflictions, but He commands us to resort to Him and rejoice in Him, in spite of them. He does command us to let the affliction do the work within us that He desires.

All of us have spilled some chocolate milk in our days. We've all made some messes. We all have "ways" that need to be examined—areas where God desires growth and greater maturity. We all need to be purged and pruned to greater fruitfulness.

Be thankful God doesn't turn around and pour out His anger. Be transparent with Him. Practice confessing—acknowledging your sin. Let Him examine your heart and expose your blind spots. And in this season of suffering, let the Potter shape the clay. Let the nurturing work of God purge you that you might become a vessel fit for the Master's use.

Many things are uncertain right now, but of one thing you can be absolutely certain!

God is not pouring out His anger upon you. He is *growing* you in His grace—*favoring* you. And He has nothing less than your absolute best in mind, both now, and for all of eternity!

How Firm a Foundation

How firm a foundation, ye saints of the Lord,
Is laid for your faith in His excellent word!
What more can He say than to you He hath said—
To you who for refuge to Jesus have fled?

"Fear not, I am with thee, oh, be not dismayed,
For I am thy God, and will still give thee aid;
I'll strengthen thee, help thee, and cause thee to stand,
Upheld by My gracious, omnipotent hand.

"When through fiery trials thy pathway shall lie,
My grace, all-sufficient, shall be thy supply;
The flame shall not harm thee; I only design
Thy dross to consume and thy gold to refine.

"The soul that on Jesus doth lean for repose,
I will not, I will not, desert to his foes;
That soul, though all hell should endeavor to shake,
I'll never, no never, no never forsake."

—JOHN KEITH

EIGHT
BE STRONG AND WORK

...be strong...all ye people of the land, saith the LORD, and
work: for I am with you, saith the LORD of hosts:
—HAGGAI 2:4

CHEMOTHERAPY AND I HAVE DEVELOPED A LOVE/
hate relationship. I love it from a distance! Throughout
treatment I've tried to think of ways to avoid chemo. Somehow
this is therapeutic. Here are my top five ideas:

1. *Hang around sick people and breathe deeply*—borrowing a
virus can make the body too weak to receive treatment.

2. *Flee the country*—I have missionary friends in a lot
of places. And I'm sure there are smugglers in Southern
California who could smuggle me across the border!

3. *Enter a witness protection program*—assuming a new
identity and moving to Idaho might do the trick.

4. *Tell them I have jury duty*—they've made it impossible to
get out of that now. When I told the jury office I had cancer,

the lady asked "how bad" then would only grant a temporary postponement! That's just wrong.

5. Find a disguise and hang out at the donut shop all day—I really believe cinnamon rolls kill cancer. I just need to begin a case study. Seriously, has anyone studied this? If fruit is that important, I'll throw in an apple fritter too.

Speaking of fruit, the doctor did tell me that it's good to eat more fruit, so today began with blueberry Pop Tarts. For lunch—peach ice cream. And after dinner—a strawberry Blow Pop.

A Strange New Year

As the new year kicked into gear, so did the pace of ministry and family life. The general treatment routine played out in two-week cycles—a bad week followed by a better week. God allowed us to spend several days with friends on the beautiful central California coast. It was a needed retreat in the middle of the trial. The winter weather was a consistent reminder of the cold season of life, and I often found my heart longing for spring—both practically and physically. The spring meant the end of chemo, and hopefully full remission from this dreaded disease. A consistent prayer request was, "Lord, please help May to arrive quickly!"

At about the mid-treatment point, one of the most challenging aspects of chemo was the "Anticipatory Nausea."

This is the nausea experienced because of the psychological triggers related to the chemo process. I call it "Associative Nausea"—first because there's nothing to "anticipate" about it, and second because it's really about associations.

The oddest things would somehow trigger a memory of the chemo experience and bring instant nausea and gagging. Often it was smells—like hand sanitizer or strong perfumes. At other times it was visual—like any red colored drink (one of my chemo chemicals is red in color). And at other times it was just the thought of the treatment experience. Honestly, even writing about chemo in this book has often been a noxious experience.

It was also about this time that the hair loss kicked in. Hair has been leaving my head for many years, but by late January 2011, it was starting to look pretty patchy, so I finally took the plunge. Armed with a razor and shaving cream and a few family witnesses looking on, I went to work. First step— mohawk-ville—"The Last of the Mohicans." A moment later, I emerged with a radiant, white glow that you wouldn't exactly call angelic.

In response from friends, I have heard that I look like everyone from Mr. Clean to Shrek to my father and grandfather. To me, I just looked like Uncle Fester—especially with the dark circles under my eyes. My primary comment about baldness was quite simple—"my head is cold!"

For most of the family, the baldness was a bit emotional—
sort of an exclamation point on the word "cancer." But my
daughter's response cheered us all up. I went into the office
for a few hours, and called her out of class to show her my
head. To my delight and surprise, she walked in, broke into
a huge smile, giggled cutely, and said, "Hey—you look cool!"
Then she came over to my desk and started rubbing my head.
She laughed and went with it. That did my heart a lot of good.

Tempted to Be Discouraged

At this point in the trial I really hit a wall. I was tempted
to pout. Having to be withdrawn from people, from
ministry, and from the normal routines of life was starting
to discourage me at a new level. The new year brought with
it a lot of ministry excitement and anticipation. And quite
honestly, I love being in the ministry. I love going into the
office every day and serving the Lord. Cancer was killing
that, and it was a tough thing to accept. My functional life
was reduced by more than 50 percent, and this had to be
divided between work and family, which meant my ministry
life felt minuscule—not to mention that I felt like a large
burden to those around me.

Treatment weeks were keeping me in bed for the better
part of five days, and even after that I was weak and pathetic
for another five. Everyone around me was encouraging and

supportive, but the temptation was to simply feel like a loser. At times I wondered if normalcy would ever return, if I would ever be able to serve like I once had, and what would happen if not. While not angry or accusing God, I often asked Him, "Lord, why? What are you doing? Why have you sidelined me?" There really weren't any answers to those questions except, "Wait and hope."

ENEMIES—LETHARGY & APATHY

The danger of these emotional wrestlings was *lethargy* and *apathy*. This trial possibly represented a significant opportunity to sink into despair over my inabilities. After twenty-one years of very busy, active, and enjoyable family and ministry life, suddenly I'm sitting on the sidelines and out of play for the rest of the season. Spiritual atrophy could have begun to set in. There was a real possibility of backsliding and becoming apathetic. It would have been easy and tempting to withdraw into a self-focused emotional cocoon and lose heart for the vital matters of life—after all, what good was I any way?

It was in the middle of this season of physical, emotional, and spiritual weakness that God led me to another very powerful portion of Scripture.

Haggai was a prophet and servant of God during a very critical time in Israel's history. The period of exile that began with Nebuchadnezzar in the book of Daniel had come to an end through the prophesied reign of the Persian king, Cyrus, whom we studied earlier. The children of Israel had been set free and allowed to return to Jerusalem. Along with their return, God commanded them to rebuild the temple.

The work of rebuilding began, but it was not easy. There was much resistance, and over time, the work ceased. The people grew disheartened and lethargic. They disengaged from their mission and forgot God's promises of provision. For a myriad of reasons, they were discouraged in the process and national forward momentum halted. They began second-guessing God and rationalizing amongst themselves that "The time is not come, the time that the LORD's house should be built" (Haggai 1:2).

Furthermore, their priorities were wrong. They were caring for themselves and fighting for their own survival, but God's house laid waste. Because of this, they were missing out on the favor, blessing, and provision of God. He had released them from captivity with specific instructions to return home and return to Him. He wanted to be their first priority, and survival their second. If they would keep Him in first place, He would insure their survival. God never intends for *survival* to be our first priority.

The plan was simple—*keep God first and He will keep you*. Rebuild His name and His house first—glorify Him. And in so doing, God will favor you and provide in all the other aspects of re-establishing your life in Israel. But they forgot God, and all the rest of life became a struggle. With survival as their first priority, survival became all but *impossible*. They faced drought, famine, pestilence, financial woes, and resistance from enemies. And in all of these trying experiences, they lost hope and purpose. They melted down into spiritual apathy.

God Works through Weakness

It was in the middle of this national despair that God spoke through Haggai and Zechariah—two of four men whom He used to stir the people back to action. Let's discover what God said to this down-trodden group of people:

> Then spake Haggai the LORD'S messenger in the LORD'S message unto the people, saying, I am with you, saith the LORD.—HAGGAI 1:13

God reminded the people that He was with them! God Almighty was on their side, ready to accomplish His work according to His purpose. Then in chapter 2 we read:

> Yet now be strong, O Zerubbabel, saith the LORD; and be strong, O Joshua, son of Josedech, the high priest; and be strong, all ye people of the land, saith the LORD, and work: for I am with you, saith the LORD of hosts: According to the word that I covenanted with you when

ye came out of Egypt, so my spirit remaineth among you: fear ye not.—HAGGAI 2:4–5

Be strong and work. Remember, this was a weakened group of people. They were lacking strength, resources, and defenses. They were vulnerable and disheartened—giving up hope. They could have easily answered back to God, "Work on what? With what? We are barely surviving!" They could have easily reasoned themselves into continued defeat. But God's voice commanded them to action. He challenged them to rise up and act in faith.

Three times in this one verse God says, "Be strong!"— "Be resolute, courageous, firm! Be hardened in your determination! Be strengthened in your confidence in God! You can't do it alone, but I am with you!" Be strong and work. The word *work* simply means "to accomplish, to execute, to act."

To paraphrase a bit, God's Word is essentially saying, "Take your eyes off of your limitations and obstacles, stop focusing on survival—focus on God. Lift your heart from discouragement to Divinity. Place your eyes back on the providential. Be confident and strengthened in God, and move forward with action! Stop thinking about what you can't do, and start doing what you can. God's Spirit is with you, and He will accomplish His work by His power, through you."

Thankfully, the people heard the voices of Haggai, Zechariah, Zerubbabel (the governor), and Joshua (the high priest). They were stirred to spiritual revival and obedience, and God completed the work—both in them and through them. He infused them with divine courage and provided them with divine resources. To His glory, a great work was done through very weak people.

> Then Zerubbabel the son of Shealtiel, and Joshua the son of Josedech, the high priest, with all the remnant of the people, obeyed the voice of the LORD their God, and the words of Haggai the prophet, as the LORD their God had sent him, and the people did fear before the LORD.—HAGGAI 1:12

BE STRONG AND WORK

Off script times are weak times. Trials bring the temptation to be melancholy toward the high-value aspects of life. For many years you may have cruised along with focused priorities, keeping God first, but suddenly the storm threatens to derail those focused passions. Suddenly the hardship can cause you to question your calling. Complacency can slowly creep into the heart.

Like the children of Israel, God used Haggai to speak to me in such a moment of discouragement. Questions swirled in my mind. Should I step completely out of ministry for eight months? Should I resign so someone else can step into my responsibilities? What good am I to anybody at this time? What could God possibly do through my life when I'm so incapacitated? The list goes on. The accuser was aggressive.

Ironically, the very questions themselves are rooted in a subtle kind of pride and false assumption. The logic assumes that I have so much more to offer God in health than I do in sickness. False. I have nothing to offer God except a sinful life, either way. It's a miracle of grace that He allows us to serve Him at all. Any good fruit or positive outcome from our service is due to God's grace, not our efforts, or health, or strength. It's all of God.

It was through all these reminders that God said to my heart, through Haggai, "Be strong, and work. My spirit is with you."

To be transparent, I reasoned, "Work on what? With what? How? I have no strength. I have no energy. I'm sitting on the sidelines. You have rendered me useless for the moment."

Yet with relentless persistence, He kept repeating that verse over and over in my heart: "Be strong and work." A hundred times that day, those words recycled through my mind. He was saying, "It's always been all *my doing* anyway! You are no *less* useful to Me today than you were in health. As always, *I'll do what you can't.* As always, I'll accomplish something you can't comprehend. I'll work when you can't—

but you be strong and work. Do the little that you can with the little that you have."

What do you do when God rewrites your life?

Decision eight:
BE STRONG AND WORK

Do the little that you can, with the little that you have, to glorify God and serve Him. He will do the rest.

Don't sweat what you can't do—that's in God's hands. Don't despair over the past—that's gone. Don't disengage in discouragement—that's destructive. God has placed you in a weakened moment, but that doesn't mean He has stopped working, and it doesn't mean you are useless.

Press forward. Don't pause, rethink, doubt, or reconsider. Engage with God's purpose in whatever capacity He enables you, and leave the outcome to Him.

A GREATER GLORY

I must confess, I don't understand this. In the middle of this trial, I still feel relatively useless—and I'm sure you do too. My contribution to the lives of people and the work of

Christ seems so pathetic and insignificant. From the world of busyness I once traveled, to the world of weakness where I now reside, human calculations would only be depressing. But God's economy works differently. In God's scale, what I've had to offer Him has *always* been pathetic. Any good from our lives is always exceedingly glorifying to God—for we are dust.

The off script season is simply a time when God's greater glory is magnified through your greater weakness.

I wish I could tell you there is great evidence that God is doing something through me. He's doing plenty *within* me, but I can't point to some significant outcome of this trial—not yet. I may never be able to in this life—that isn't the point. This is a "by faith" section of this book. It's a "wait and see" chapter. The only reason I know God is working, is because that is His nature and character. He promises that in our weakness He is strong (2 Corinthians 12:9).

He promises that our greater weakness allows Him to do a greater work. That's what He promised through Haggai:

> *The glory of this latter house shall be greater than of the former, saith the LORD of hosts...*—HAGGAI 2:9

Think about that. God's glory would be greater through the weakened state of His people. He doesn't promise *they* will be greater. He's not glorifying *them*, He's glorifying *Himself!*

And through the greater weakness, He receives greater glory. What an amazing promise and an amazing process!

Your life and mine were created to bring God glory. This is why He redeemed us. This is why He blesses us. This is why He calls and uses us. He desires and deserves to be glorified before men, and chooses you as the vessel.

Stop and consider for a moment the profound concept that *anything* you do in this life could possibly bring glory and pleasure to the God of the universe. If that isn't mind blowing enough, step back and consider your *trial*. God has chosen to weaken you. It's painful. It's unpleasant. It's not something you would ever choose. But as the Creator, He intends to use this weakened state to somehow bring greater glory to Himself. It's not yours or mine to figure out how. It's simply ours to be the vessels of that glory—to allow it to happen by God's Spirit.

Through all of your pain and hardship—if you don't become lethargic and cease in the calling that God has given you—God will receive greater glory!

Again, two words come to mind. *Worth it!*

A Glimmer of Glory

During the first days of this trial, God gave me just a glimmer of how He could use something so terrible as cancer for His own glory.

A few days after diagnosis, I sat down and wrote a lengthy blog post to friends and family. It was the easiest way to let everyone know what was going on. I took the liberty to explain our response, and to explain our foundation and hope in the Lord. To my surprise, several people forwarded that letter to their own friends and family that were dealing with trials.

A few days later, I received an email from a Marine stationed in Germany. This young man was preparing to go to war in Afghanistan, and he was afraid of dying. Somehow he had read my post, and he asked me how I could face death with such peace and confidence.

Late at night, I read his email to my wife. We were both amazed and touched. Then, I sent him an e-book called *Done* that I had written about trusting Christ as Saviour. I asked him to read it and write me back.

The next morning, the first email in my inbox was from this same Marine. He had read *Done* that very night, and had personally prayed to trust Christ as Saviour. He was so happy to write and tell me of his decision. What an awesome blessing! Several days later, one of his friends also trusted Christ.

There are many things in life that are more valuable than life itself. God's glory is one of those things. The salvation of a soul is another. In the midst of my distress, half a world away, God was using that distress to work in the heart of two young men who needed to be saved. I can't explain that. I can't understand it. How and why God ordains these things is a mystery. But I thank God that He gave me just a glimpse of how He uses hardship for His greater glory.

No Place to Hide

Why journal this crazy experience on a blog or in a book? Frankly, I wonder sometimes. Who really cares? Why would my story matter? Millions of people have similar stories. In fact, I've started and stopped writing this book half a dozen times. The thing that compels me to pick it back up is that perhaps God could use it in some small way.

Cancer has been a humiliating process. In a large church, it's all but impossible to "privately" deal with cancer. So, for whatever reason, God has ordained to make this trial a public spectacle for others to view. Uncomfortable? Sure. In fact, the first time I walked onto the platform to lead singing with no hair, I wanted to crawl under the carpet. (Merely my pathetic pride.) But somehow God keeps saying, "I can be glorified and others edified through this."

The only correct response is, "Okay, Lord—help Yourself."

Oswald Chambers wrote in My Utmost for His Highest:

> There is no such thing as a private life, or a place to hide
> in this world, for a man or woman who is intimately
> aware of and shares in the sufferings of Jesus Christ.

God divides the private life of His saints and makes it a highway for the world on one hand and for Himself on the other. No human being can stand that unless he is identified with Jesus Christ. We are not sanctified for ourselves. We are called into intimacy with the Gospel, and things happen that appear to have nothing to do with us. But God is getting us into fellowship with Himself. Let Him have His way. If you refuse, you will be of no value to God in His redemptive work in the world, but will be a hindrance and a stumbling block.

The first thing God does is get us grounded on strong reality and truth. He does this until our cares for ourselves individually have been brought into submission to His way for the purpose of His redemption. Why shouldn't we experience heartbreak? Through those doorways God is opening up ways of fellowship with His Son. Most of us collapse at the first grip of pain. We sit down at the door of God's purpose and enter a slow death through self-pity. And all the so-called Christian sympathy of others helps us to our deathbed. But God will not. He comes with the grip of the pierced hand of His Son, as if to say, "Enter into fellowship with Me; arise and shine." If God can accomplish His purposes in this world through a broken heart, then why not thank Him for breaking yours?

Jonathan Edwards, the great preacher and theologian whom God used to bring revival to colonial America, wrote in similar fashion:

> *I claim no right to myself, no right to this understanding, this will, these affections that are in me. Neither do I have any right to this body or its members, no right to this tongue, to these hands, feet, ears or eyes. I have given myself clear away and not retained anything of my own.*
>
> *I have been to God this morning and told Him I have given myself wholly to Him, I have given every power so that for the future I claim no right to myself in any respect. I have expressly promised Him, for by His grace I will not fail. I take Him as my whole portion and felicity, looking upon nothing else as any part of my happiness.*
>
> *His law is the constant rule of my obedience. I will fight with all my might against the world, the flesh and the devil to the end of my life. I will adhere to the faith of the Gospel however hazardous and difficult the profession and practice of it may be. I pray God for the sake of others to look on this as self-dedication.*
>
> *Henceforth, I am not to act in any respect as my own. I shall act as my own if I ever make use of any of my powers to do anything that is not to the glory of God or to fail to make the glorifying of Him my whole and entire business. If I murmur in the least at affliction, if I*

am in any way uncharitable, if I revenge my own case, if I do anything purely to please myself or omit anything because it is a great denial, if I trust myself, if I take any praise for any good which Christ does by me, or if I am in any way proud, I shall act as my own and not God's. But I purpose to be absolutely His.

Off script times make you want to run and hide. I don't mean rest and restore (those times are needful)—I mean retreat from God's purpose and from the public humiliation of being weakened. Weak times kick a major dent in your pride. Whatever self-assurance or personal agenda there was, it's been given a major adjustment downward. But these are very good things. They allow God to have greater glory.

Whatever you do, don't become lethargic or complacent towards the work God has given you to do. You may need to rest. You may be physically incapacitated. You may be utterly weakened. However incapable you feel, determine to do *what* you can, *when* you can, with the little you have.

Choose to declare the grace of God from the grip of pain.

Your trial is a sacred trust from God to you. Refuse to collapse at the door of purpose only to enter the slow death of self-pity, as Chambers referred to it.

Choose rather to *be strong and work*—for God's Spirit is most assuredly with you!

A MIGHTY FORTRESS IS OUR GOD

A mighty fortress is our God, a bulwark never failing;
Our helper He amid the flood of mortal ills prevaling.
For still our ancient foe doth seek to work us woe;
His craft and power are great, and armed with cruel hate,
On earth is not his equal.

Did we in our own strength confide, our striving would be losing,
Were not the right man on our side, the man of God's own choosing.
Dost ask who that may be? Christ Jesus, it is He;
Lord Sabaoth, His name, from age to age the same,
And He must win the battle.

And though this world, with devils filled, should threaten to undo us,
We will not fear, for God hath willed His truth to triumph through us.
The prince of darkness grim, we tremble not for him;
His rage we can endure, for lo, his doom is sure;
One little word shall fell him.

That word above all earthly powers, no thanks to them, abideth;
The Spirit and the gifts are ours, thru Him who with us sideth.
Let goods and kindred go, this mortal life also;
The body they may kill; God's truth abideth still;
His kingdom is forever.

—MARTIN LUTHER

NINE
LOVE YOUR OWN

...having loved his own which were in the world,
he loved them unto the end. —JOHN 13:1

MID-TREATMENT HIT IN FEBRUARY—A TIME I HAD greatly anticipated. Hodgkin's lymphoma is not as aggressive as other cancers. I was told that Hodgkin's responds very quickly to treatment. Although, that positive information was tempered when I regularly visited an online Hodgkin's community with my questions. There were plenty of difficult stories there—long treatments, recurrence, and occasionally the passing of someone who had fought long against this cancer. As hopeful as I was, these stories made me cautious.

It was finally time to schedule another CT scan and PET scan to discover what sort of progress was being made against the tumors. I was back in the big green chair for treatment number seven when the doctor stepped in holding the CT scan report:

"How are you, Mr. Tough Man?" he asked. (Don't forget the Nigerian accent when you read that.)

I smiled—"Not so tough today."

Since the scan, I had tried not to think much about the results. There was always the chance that the tumors weren't responding, or that they didn't respond much. Thankfully, that wasn't the case as the doctor proceeded to explain.

"Progress has been extreme!" he said, "I am amazed!" The largest of my tumors, in the center of my chest, was originally 8.6 centimeters at its widest point. This was borderline for what is considered "large" or bulky disease. Not good. That day the same tumor, at its largest point, measured only 1.5 centimeters. This was a major answer to prayer! In the doctor's words, "This is miraculous!"

All the tumors showed the same progress. Was I out of the woods yet? No. The road ahead was still long and uncertain, but I was thankful. I sat in the chemo chair and brushed away tears of gratitude for about an hour. I guess I wasn't emotionally prepared to receive such a great report.

The next big hurdle was the PET scan, nearly a month later. This is the real cancer test—the one that shows dark spots where cancer exists. The PET scan technician was a Christian, and before the scan we shared our testimonies. As

I stepped out of the machine about forty-five minutes later, I asked when the doctor would have results.

"In a couple of days," he said, "but, wow, it looks pretty good to me!" He pointed to the screen in front of him.

"Is that me?" I asked.

"Yep—it looks 100 percent to me!" he said. I leaned in and looked at the image. It was completely different than the one I had seen back in October. My upper body in the image was completely clear of any black areas!

The technician looked at me, smiled, and said, "Praise Jesus, huh?"

Well, that was the understatement of the year! I hadn't expected to get results until later in the week. This was amazing news! I stepped into the waiting room, threw my arms in the air, hugged Dana, and told her the news. Then we went to lunch, fought back the tears, and thanked the Lord.

I met with my doctor again the next Thursday and he shared the report with me. It reads "...complete resolution of PET abnormalities..."—medical terms for "this scan doesn't show any cancer!"

What did this all mean? While there could be some remaining cancer cells in my body, there are no detectable, visible cancerous regions. This was a miraculous answer to prayer that breathed new life into my will to fight. The remaining treatments were still required, and the road would be tough, but at least healing was under way. I still ask the Lord daily for "no recurrence" and I'm still cautious in my optimism, as a battle with cancer could return at any time. But for the moment, we thank the Lord for answered prayer. It appeared that a light was flickering at the end of this horrible tunnel.

To celebrate, we took the kids away for three days at the end of Spring Break. We rested, read, shopped, and laughed—good memories that fell on "feeling good" days.

23-19!

Until March of 2011, I thought shingles were things that you put on the roof of your house. That was until my son Larry walked into my bedroom one Saturday evening and said, "Hey, you have spots on your back."

I looked and then jumped online to find out what was wrong. Chemo does a lot of weird things, so I expected an unexplainable rash. What I discovered was "shingles!" By Monday, chemo was postponed yet again (thank you, Lord!) and I was prescribed five large pills per day. Everyone told me this was going to be painful and itchy, but four days into it, it wasn't so bad. I was too optimistic. Somebody should have told me to buckle up—there was definitely a blasting zone ahead!

That week, my son Lance started declaring a 23-19! (In case you are not "Monsters, Inc." educated, a 23-19 is what the CDC declares whenever a monster has been contaminated by a child.) If my kids had protective suits, they would have worn them. If they could have put me behind a curtain and hosed me down with disinfectant, they would have— laughing all the way.

I was essentially quarantined. Dana threatened to send me to the guest room. Haylee refused to hug me closer than ten inches. She would pause, look at me cautiously, and then select a safe spot on my head to gently pat as she backed away. Then she rushed to the sink to wash her hands. Can't you just feel the love!

For several days I tried to think of one name that combined Hodgkin's and Shingles—like Shodgkins... or Shingkins... or Hodggles... Shingphoma? Lymphgles? Nothing seemed to work right.

DANA'S DANGEROUS CURE

After about a week, shingles had declared an all-out mutiny. The sores were healing, but the itching and weird nerve pain on my back and chest was driving away my last remnants of sanity. My new best friend became a small bamboo back scratcher that Dana picked up at the store. And I started seriously considering building a bed of nails to sleep on.

For a solid month I didn't sleep longer than an hour at a time. The bathroom counter was laden with every kind of itch cream, spray, gel, and ointment we could find—and none of it helped for more than twenty minutes. This was just long enough to fall back asleep, only to wake up on the edge of sanity again.

Finally, Dana decided to go online and search for some home remedies. She found a few, and after a quick trip to the store, told me to take my shirt off. As I did, she pulled out a bottle of Apple Cider Vinegar and a small container of natural itch potion that she must have purchased from a group of traveling gypsies. A few moments later she was spraying me down.

At first, I started craving fish and chips—you know, the vinegar smell. Then, suddenly everything changed! Not only did I smell like a giant fish stick, but my body was burning like I had been dropped into a deep fryer! She may as well have doused me with kerosene and set me on fire. I started jumping and dancing around the bathroom, begging for mercy and trying to think of what to do. Finally, I jumped into the cold shower. It was then I saw Dana—literally doubled over and holding her stomach with laughter! In between gasps for breath and shreaks of pain, all I could say was, "Oh sure—I see how it is—laugh it up…." She did.

It was then that I began to understand how some "natural cures" work. The cure is so much worse than the problem, that before too long, you're begging to return to your original condition. So a few moments later, after Dana's combustible concoction was rinsed off, I was only too happy to return to my normal itching and burning. And that will be the last time I allow anyone to try an "internet cure" on me—that's for sure!

The next night, she was putting a new cream on my back— this time only a small dab for fear that it might be painful. She was being very careful. As soon as she touched my back I screamed with frantic and traumatic intensity. She jumped back, gasped, and began to apologize... and then I said, "Just kidding...." It wasn't exactly revenge, but it sure felt good. Then it was me who was doubled over with laughter—but only for a few seconds, because I had to scratch my back!

All in all, this was just another funny part of the journey. I started praying that the shingles would depart and enter into a herd of swine or something. But in retrospect, the shingles turned out to be a gift on a number of levels. The Lord knew we needed a break from treatments, and shingles made that happen.

What Matters Most

The point of these stories is this—while our trial has been filled with hard moments, it's also been filled with loving moments, funny moments, and family moments. The trial has served to draw our family closer to the Lord and to each other. Through this season we've shared more comical situations and side-splitting laughter than I could possibly recount. We've always enjoyed laughing at each other, but usually I have the upper hand in picking on everybody else. The last six months have brought sweet revenge for the rest of the family. Now I'm the object of laughter—and yes, I deserve it.

God has used this mixture of heavy and funny experiences to drive home another very important principle about what really matters most! He has caused our family to love each other more fervently through the trial.

Have you ever rushed through your day at a frantic pace, crossing off as many things on your to-do list as possible? Have you ever finished a busy day, collapsed into bed, and wondered what you did of value that day? Have you ever sensed, deep inside, that you're getting a lot of "stuff" done, but something is still missing? It's easy to do a lot of good things with our time and life, but to miss the really important things—the things that matter most. And when we do, our conscience is unsettled.

Needless to say, cancer and its related dynamics has changed our schedules and lives dramatically. The whole experience has required us to refine, refocus, and remain fixed on the things that truly do matter in family and ministry.

About three months into this battle, on an evening when I had some energy, I said to Dana, "I really believe the Lord wants me to take Haylee out for a date tonight. I can sense in her heart and spirit that she needs time with me." I have felt bad that my kids have had to watch me suffer through the effects of chemo, and often more so for Haylee because she's the youngest. Must be hard for a ten year old to process all of that.

Later that evening, to her delight, I told Haylee I had a surprise! She smiled and, of course, asked, "What is it?" "I can't tell you... just go get ready for a date!" With that, she excitedly began to prepare. She loves to look her best for our dates. Her delightful anticipation assured me that this was a very good decision!

A few moments later we were in the car, hand in hand, looking forward to time together. We started at Macy's to look for a dress—no luck. Then we made our way to a restaurant in the mall where we shared a meal. Already the look on her face implied a peaceful heart, a settled spirit, and great contentment in being with her father.

We talked, and talked...and talked. We talked about the problems of growing up, the challenges of 5th grade social politics, and understanding hard things in life. We talked about cancer and how she was doing with this. We even talked a little bit about boys (Uggh!). After dinner, I had some bone pain from the Neupogen, and was finding it a little painful to walk.

"Come on Dad, you don't feel well, we can go to the car and go home." I think Haylee had been clued in by mom to "take care of me."

"No, no... I'm fine... come on, we gotta go find a dress." And so we proceeded to Dillard's.

It was almost closing time, but Dillard's was a gold mine of new little girl dresses, and within about twenty minutes the dress was purchased and we were beginning our long, limpy walk through the mall and back to the car.

As we left the store, I gently put my arm around her and said, "This is one of my very most favorite things to do in all of my life—take you out to eat and buy you a pretty dress!"

She sweetly said, "Thank you."

Haylee was very quiet for the next several minutes of our walk. I wondered what she was thinking. Then, out of nowhere, about halfway to the car, she let go of my hand, hugged me with both arms, closed her eyes, and said with a long sigh, "I really, really love you...."

It was precious. Unforgettable. The look on her face and the sweet tone in her voice seemed to say, "My heart is SO OK right now, I can't even put it into words!"

It was then that the Holy Spirit said to me, "This is the most important thing you did today!" I thought back through the day. The morning was spent in bed, trying to answer emails and feign productivity amidst feeling sick. The afternoon enabled me to get into the office for a couple of hours to sign letters, have a couple of meetings, and try to get a little work done. But the value of the day—the real significance of the whole day was found in these final few hours with Haylee. Why?

Well, first because she is dependent upon me. She's my daughter. She, along with the rest of my family, is my most valuable, most significant, most precious ministry. My four family members truly are the only people on the planet that are actually dependent upon me. The rest of the world is not. These precious people are dependent upon me in every way.

Simply put, the most important things any of us do on any day are those things we do to love, care for, nurture, and provide for our families. How can we expect our kids to fall in love with God and grow in His grace if we aren't falling in love with them and showing His grace?

Second, because she is a person. Her heart, her emotions, her struggles, her feelings, her questions, her burdens matter; and her mother and I are God's gifts to her to walk her through all these new life experiences. She's never been there! It's called parenting, and what a gift it is! Sometimes I think that we forget our children are people, new people who are experiencing everything for the first time! They are people who matter to God, and they are the most important people in your life, if you are a parent. No one else and nothing else should trump your relationship with your family, I don't care who it is, what they demand, or what kind of pressure they place upon you. Nothing trumps your family!

When we got home that night, Dana instructed Haylee to get ready for bed. A few moments later, Dana came into our room and said to me, "She's a different person! She's at peace. She's whole. She's gentle and responsive. It's like these last three hours with you untied every knot in her heart!" I could sense it also. Haylee was a different person, because Dad spent some time loving her. (And by the way, it wasn't about the dress, it was about the connection of hearts.)

JESUS' PRIORITIES

In John 13, we arrive at a very important evening in the life of Jesus. This is His final evening of life—His hour had come, and He fully knew it. He is about to be betrayed, brutally beaten, and crucified for the sins of mankind.

There is no way I could adequately *understand*, much less *describe* the spiritual and emotional intensity that Jesus faced on this night. Matthew 26:37 says that Jesus was "sorrowful and very heavy." In the next verse Jesus said, "My soul is exceeding sorrowful, even unto death." In the next, He asks the Heavenly Father, "…if it be possible, let this cup pass from me…." Mark 14:33 states that Jesus was "sore amazed" and "very heavy." Luke 22:43 describes that God sent an angel from Heaven to strengthen him. Verse 44 says he was in "agony" and sweat "as it were great drops of blood."

What would you choose to do the evening before your death? How would you respond if you knew you would soon be experiencing these descriptives? What did Jesus do just moments before these accounts? John 13 describes it for us:

> *Now before the feast of the passover, when Jesus knew that his hour was come that he should depart out of this world unto the Father, having loved his own which were in the world, he loved them unto the end.*—JOHN 13:1

> *Jesus knowing that the Father had given all things into his hands, and that he was come from God, and went to God; He riseth from supper, and laid aside his garments; and took a towel, and girded himself. After that he poureth water into a bason, and began to wash the disciples' feet, and to wipe them with the towel wherewith he was girded.*—JOHN 13:3–5

Before His death, Jesus shared a meal with those He loved. He then rose to serve them by washing their feet with a towel and bason. And then He began to share His final instructions with them. He challenged them to serve one another as He did:

> Ye call me Master and Lord: and ye say well; for so I am. If I then, your Lord and Master, have washed your feet; ye also ought to wash one another's feet. For I have given you an example, that ye should do as I have done to you. Verily, verily, I say unto you, The servant is not greater than his lord; neither he that is sent greater than he that sent him. If ye know these things, happy are ye if ye do them.—JOHN 13:13–17

He commanded them to love one another as He loved:

> A new commandment I give unto you, That ye love one another; as I have loved you, that ye also love one another. By this shall all men know that ye are my disciples, if ye have love one to another. —JOHN 13:34–35

His heart was focused on those He loved—preparing them, loving them, and investing into them. Even in His final hours of life, He served. He expended Himself for others. When He could have reasonably stopped engaging in the close relationships of His earthly life, He didn't. In the midst of overwhelming circumstances, He found the ability to love people.

What do you do when God rewrites your life?

Decision nine:
LOVE YOUR OWN

Passionately cherish your family and love them as Christ loves them. Make every good day special!

Jesus' priority was people. He loved His own to the end. The challenge to love as He loves is not an easy one. He loves perfectly, unconditionally, and infinitely. That's a tall order to match.

In the off script times, there are many things outside of our control—but loving people is something we can always do. Love those God has placed within your reach—that's what Jesus would do. When you're tempted to withdraw in isolation and melt down in self-pity—look around and choose rather to express Christ-like love to those closest to you.

Trials require times of quiet restoration or soulful consternation alone with God. Protect those times—as we already discussed. But as God gives the grace and strength, turn your heart toward those around you and genuinely, sincerely, earnestly love them.

CHASING DAYLIGHT

We tend to live like tomorrow is a guarantee. Off script times provide a cold and stark reminder that this assumption is false. You may not have another chance to love those closest to you. Your time to express that love and care may genuinely be limited—or suddenly gone. The call of God is to love people as though this is the last opportunity to do so. The challenge is to maintain every relationship, through every moment, as whole, healthy, and loving as you would want it to be when you leave this Earth.

We live in a busy age. This is a day when most people live with little to no margins in life. The spaces on our calendar that jobs and commitments don't fill, we quickly fill with everything else—from soccer practices to music recitals to Facebook. And for all of our urgent busyness and frantic pace to "get it all done," we end our days with a nagging conscience. While we may be updated on everybody else's recent news, perhaps we missed what matters the most—loving those closest to us. We pay a high price when we neglect relationships.

I read an interesting book at the beginning of this battle. It was called *Chasing Daylight*. It wasn't a Christian book, but it was written by a highly successful CEO who was diagnosed with three fast-growing, cancerous brain tumors. Sadly, he was given three months to live. The book chronicles how he decided to live his last three months of life.

This was a man whose life was consumed with success—earning money, making his company successful, and enjoying all the perks of wealth. And he was good at it. He had multiple homes, chartered private jets, and enjoyed everything his heart desired. He provided well for his family. But from the moment of diagnosis, none of that mattered. When given three months to live, there was only one thing that mattered—relationships. He spent his last three months doing what he called "unwinding relationships"—spending time closing his relationships with people he loved and appreciated. Suddenly, money and success faded, and life was all about relationships—people!

This was God's challenge to me—through John 13—*love your own*. Help them through this. Nurture them, care for them, keep them focused on Christ. Pray with them, play with them, laugh with them. Many are the days when I haven't had the ability or strength to fully engage, but for those in-between times—the good days sure have been special.

Sick days come and go, and the Holy Spirit's first prompting as He's drawing me out of the chemo-cave has been something like this:

"Love your own. Make today special for your wife, your sons, your daughter. Cherish them and honor them like it's your last chance. Then, be available to people who need encouragement. Do what you can to love the people that God places within your reach."

I'm not saying I've done a good job at it. In fact, I've failed more than I want to admit. But I've tried to obey His prompting. It's a day by day, moment by moment quest. It's easy to fall off the horse—to be punchy, grumpy, or irritable. Off script times can do that to you. They can turn you into Oscar the Grouch—and even make you feel justified in being so. You can rationalize—*don't they know what kind of pressure I'm under? Don't they know how horrible I feel? I have a right to be insensitive and irritable!* But I encourage you to get back on the horse. Don't let it happen, and when it does, *apologize.* Love your own.

Love Like There's No Tomorrow

Study the life and ministry of Jesus. His days weren't spent processing projects or checking off His to-do list. (Though most of us must do some of that.) His days were spent touching the lives of people. He lived in balance—resting when necessary, walking with His Heavenly Father, and giving Himself to people. He was never in a hurry. He lived with plenty of margin. (He walked nearly everywhere He went.) He never let urgency determine His agenda. His life, ministry, and daily agenda were driven by the leading of His

Father and the lives of people. With Jesus, on a practical daily level, people mattered the most.

Do people matter most in your life? Begin with the people closest to you—for they are the ones God has given to you. Then work your way out from there. Focus your life on loving, serving, and investing into people. Connect everything you do—even the task list and the projects—to the needs of people. When you plan your day and your week, begin with people. Make sure that every relationship in your life is healed and healthy. Work to keep them that way. No matter what you accomplish in life, if your relationships are broken or neglected, you are failing at what matters the most to Jesus.

How did you live your life today? What's your plan for tomorrow? Are you neglecting people for the sake of "more important things"? Are you withdrawing into your trial and rationalizing your bad attitude? Next to loving God, there's nothing more important in life than loving people.

There really may be "no tomorrow." Don't waste this moment. Love them like there is no tomorrow.

O the Deep, Deep Love of Jesus

O the deep, deep love of Jesus,
Vast, unmeasured, boundless, free!
Rolling as a mighty ocean
In its fullness over me!
Underneath me, all around me,
Is the current of Thy love
Leading onward, leading homeward
To Thy glorious rest above!

O the deep, deep love of Jesus,
Spread His praise from shore to shore!
How He loveth, ever loveth,
Changeth never, nevermore!
How He watches o'er His loved ones,
Died to call them all His own;
How for them He intercedeth,
Watcheth o'er them from the throne!

O the deep, deep love of Jesus,
Love of every love the best!
'Tis an ocean full of blessing,
'Tis a haven giving rest!
O the deep, deep love of Jesus,
'Tis a heaven of heavens to me;
And it lifts me up to glory,
For it lifts me up to Thee!

—S. Trevor Francis

TEN
STRIVE TOGETHER

...that ye stand fast in one spirit, with one mind striving together for the faith of the gospel;—PHILIPPIANS 1:27

IT IS A CHALLENGE TO FIND WORDS TO DESCRIBE how God's people have blessed our lives through this trial. It is truly an awesome privilege to claim membership in the family of God, and to experience that family in a loving, Christ-centered local church.

From the first moment of this trial to this very moment—God has surrounded us with the body of Christ, and there is no way I could adequately describe the grace, strength, and encouragement we have drawn from the love of God's people.

First, our church family at Lancaster Baptist has strengthened us in amazing and innumerable ways. Our mailbox, email boxes, and message inboxes have continually been filled with loving expressions of support, prayer, and scriptural encouragement. Our front porch has been the drop-off point for many kind expressions of love—floral arrangements, holiday treats, helpful gifts, delicious meals, and thoughtful cards.

I have missed standing in our church lobby to fellowship with people after services. Low blood counts and a suppressed immune system have required that I avoid shaking a lot of hands and spending extended time around large crowds. But every time we meet a church member in the hallway, at the doctor, or in some public place we are reminded of continual prayers on our behalf.

The young people of the student ministry have repeatedly expressed their love and encouragement. Teaching the Senior class this year has been a special treasure—and one of the few people groups with whom I've been able to enjoy fellowship. Their spirit and joy, more than a few times, has seemed like a radiant infusion of energy directly to my soul.

Then the West Coast Baptist College students have repeatedly reached out with words of encouragement and kindness. Hardly a day goes by that I don't receive a note or message from a Bible college student telling me that they pray for our family. It is humbling to be told by so many that they are praying.

Family, ministry friends, and co-laborers have continually called, written, and extended their support and prayers. The hard times have been made indescribably more bearable and endurable through the grace of so many. Only eternity will reveal what the prayers of God's people have truly accomplished in my life and family these past months.

WHY IS THIS HAPPENING?

One of the first passages of Scripture that God led me to in this trial was Philippians 1. The Apostle Paul is writing to the church at Philippi, in the midst of his own trial. And he is explaining to these young and growing Christians why hard and difficult things have happened to him. Look at his explanation:

> *But I would ye should understand, brethren, that the things which happened unto me have fallen out rather unto the furtherance of the gospel; So that my bonds in Christ are manifest in all the palace, and in all other places; And many of the brethren in the Lord, waxing confident by my bonds, are much more bold to speak the word without fear.*—PHILIPPIANS 1:12–14

To paraphrase, Paul said, "My trials are happening for the furtherance of the Gospel. You need to understand what God is doing. My bonds—my shackles—are brought about by Christ so that I can speak the Gospel in many other places— including the palace. And it doesn't stop there! Many other

Christians, seeing my bonds, are becoming more courageous to preach Christ without fear!"

God was using the trials Paul was facing, not only to give Paul a greater voice for the Gospel, but also to strengthen other Christians to proclaim Christ as well. The Apostle wanted the church to understand this as well. He wanted other Christians to see Him glorify God, whether by life or by death. See what he says a few verses later:

> For I know that this shall turn to my salvation through
> your prayer, and the supply of the Spirit of Jesus Christ,
> According to my earnest expectation and my hope, that
> in nothing I shall be ashamed, but that with all boldness,
> as always, so now also Christ shall be magnified in my
> body, whether it be by life, or by death. For to me to live
> is Christ, and to die is gain.—PHILIPPIANS 1:19–21

To paraphrase again— "I believe that I will survive this ordeal because of your prayers and God's Spirit, but even if I don't, I want to have boldness to magnify Christ—either by life or by death. Either way, I'm okay!"

And then a few verses later, from his bonds—from within his own season of suffering—he challenges them with the following verse:

> Only let your conversation be as it becometh the gospel
> of Christ: that whether I come and see you, or else be

absent, I may hear of your affairs, that ye stand fast in one spirit, with one mind striving together for the faith of the gospel;—PHILIPPIANS 1:27

Paul challenged them from his chains. Live a life becoming of the Gospel. Stand fast with one spirit. Be of one mind. Continue striving together for the faith of the Gospel. Together—as a church family—press forward in unity for the faith of Christ.

CHOOSING TO STRIVE FORWARD

Off script times can cause you to step away from God's family. Suffering can make you retreat into a proverbial corner, and start licking your own wounds. Who could blame you? After all, you've got enough to worry about with your own problems, right? Trials are a perfect time to rationalize your own backsliding.

And so, the Apostle Paul says, "Don't do it!"

Hardship is a part of the Christian faith. It is a part of the forward momentum of the Gospel. It is intricate to the growth and advancement of a local body. We need each other because all of us, at one time or another, travel through trouble. The "great fight of affliction" is woven into the fabric of mankind's mission with God. Since the beginning of time, those who love God and are called according to His purpose find themselves up against overwhelming odds and extreme circumstances—so much so that we must continually claim this verse:

> And we know that all things work together for good to them that love God, to them who are the called according to his purpose.—ROMANS 8:28

All things work together for good—why would we need to know this if the Christian life weren't difficult by design? Peter tells us not to be surprised by fiery trials, hardship, tough times. Expect them. Know they are coming. And understand their purpose.

What do you do when God rewrites your life?

Decision ten:
STRIVE TOGETHER FOR THE FAITH

Lock arms with your church family, strengthen each other, and move forward expecting God to use your hardships to further the Gospel of His kingdom.

At a time when you could be tempted to retreat, let your trial, by God's providence, somehow advance the cause of Christ. Let God use you to encourage others through your local church. *Be the church* to one another, and to the lost world—even in your "bonds."

I recognize that many off script seasons make church attendance or Christian service impossible (ie: the Apostle Paul in prison). That's not necessarily what I'm talking about. What I'm describing is more about your heart and identity as a Christian. No matter your hardship, remain a Christian with a cause—a Christian that is growing in grace with your church family for the furthering of the Gospel of Christ.

THE CARE OF THE BODY

The care and compassion of Christ, as expressed through a local church body, is truly a tangible, visible expression of the grace of God. Being on the receiving end of that expression is humbling, life-changing, and sustaining. The local church is a gift from God—purchased with the blood of Christ.

During your off script time, let that loving body minister to your needs, as the Apostle Paul let the church at Philippi minister to him. See how he describes it here:

> But I rejoiced in the Lord greatly, that now at the last your care of me hath flourished again; wherein ye were also careful, but ye lacked opportunity. Not that I speak in respect of want: for I have learned, in whatsoever state I am, therewith to be content. I know both how to be abased, and I know how to abound:

every where and in all things I am instructed both to be full and to be hungry, both to abound and to suffer need. I can do all things through Christ which strengtheneth me. Notwithstanding ye have well done, that ye did communicate with my affliction. Now ye Philippians know also, that in the beginning of the gospel, when I departed from Macedonia, no church communicated with me as concerning giving and receiving, but ye only. For even in Thessalonica ye sent once and again unto my necessity. Not because I desire a gift: but I desire fruit that may abound to your account. But I have all, and abound: I am full, having received of Epaphroditus the things which were sent from you, an odour of a sweet smell, a sacrifice acceptable, wellpleasing to God. But my God shall supply all your need according to his riches in glory by Christ Jesus.—PHILIPPIANS 4:10–19

God has added an imperfect you to an imperfect church family as a part of His perfect plan. He desires to use your church family to minister His grace to your heart. You need your church family during your trial—don't withdraw.

Then, when spring comes, and your trial subsides to some degree, you will be uniquely equipped to minister to others in need. Your church will benefit from your ministry, as the members minister one to another.

The Apostle Paul knew firsthand how the ministry of the body of Christ was essential to his own ministry, as well as the church's ministry. The functioning, healthy, Bible-centered local church is an amazing aspect of the plan of God. And it is essential that you stay connected, grafted into your local body during your great fight of affliction. Don't let the wretchedness of your adversity wrench you away from the body.

Getting the Body to Function

During this trial, physical rest has been a required priority—along with eating. On chemo, the body doesn't function properly. It doesn't sleep right, eat right, digest right, and the list goes on. As the chemical effects gradually subside, the body starts functioning again, but it's temperamental and unpredictable—especially its appetites. With cancer, you're supposed to eat healthy, but sometimes just getting your stomach to agree with anything is a challenge. So you eat what you can, when you can, often just for the calories and energy to move forward.

After getting ready in the morning, my first experience is my stomach feeling like it's in a cheese grater. Getting food into it is essential to any semblance of a decent day. And with low white blood counts, the food cravings are generally related to high protein—meat, meat, and more meat. Then cheese—lots of cheese. All kinds of cheese, and extra cheese on pizza. Then eggs—yes, dozens and dozens of eggs. It seems like most meals have in some way consisted of meat, cheese, or eggs. And then on rare occasions, the other side of my appetite sticks its head up and says, "Hey, what about salads, fruits, and vegetables." On those rare days I find a salad bar.

My solution to these cravings has often been McDonald's in the morning. On some days, I grab my computer, find a quiet corner at McDonald's, and spend the first hour of the day eating breakfast and studying or answering emails. The food puts some energy into my system, and the uninterrupted time allows my brain to establish clarity.

When the body is finally functioning well, life is good. Somewhat comically, it's been a daily challenge to get the various systems of my body to agree with one another and work in concert. Kill cancer, grow white blood cells, keep hair, digest food, breathe air, sleep soundly, think clearly, don't worry, circulate blood, taste food—it's like I'm learning how to walk and chew gum! For most people this stuff just happens without a second thought—it's all beautifully in motion.

In much the same way, the body life of a local church is meant to function beautifully in motion. When it doesn't—when strife and division reign, the body starts to weaken and grow sickly. A healthy body is a wonderful thing—both physically, and in church life.

I've been blessed to be a part of a healthy church for many years. I don't know what kind of church life you have experienced, but I know what kind of church life God desires for you to experience. He desires a healthy one—a Christ-centered, growth-oriented environment where your faith can flourish. He desires, not a perfect body, but a functioning body.

So many Christians are consumed with pettiness and pride that it prevents the body from functioning. Often a self-centered spirit infiltrates and poisons the church body, and the members turn against one another—like a body on chemo or sick with cancer. Rather than the members ministering to one another, they devour one another.

In Philippians 1, Paul is reminding the church body to stay functional. Stay unified with one spirit. Continue striving together. Peter says essentially the same thing:

> But the end of all things is at hand: be ye therefore sober, and watch unto prayer. And above all things have fervent charity among yourselves: for charity shall cover the multitude of sins. Use hospitality one to another without grudging. As every man hath received the gift, even so minister the same one to another, as good stewards of the manifold grace of God.
> —1 PETER 4:7–10

The end of all things is at hand! Stay focused on what is important. Life is filled with the petty and the paramount—

and we must constantly choose between the two. With the remaining breaths God gives me, and for the rest of my days, I want to be fully engaged in the Christ-like ministry of encouragement—ministering God's grace and seeing Him change lives with my church family.

God doesn't intend for you to strive alone—He calls you to strive together!

Blest Be the Tie That Binds

Blest be the tie that binds our hearts in Christian love;
The fellowship of kindred minds is like to that above.

Before our Father's throne we pour our ardent prayers;
Our fears, our hopes, our aims are one,
Our comforts and our cares.

We share each other's woes, our mutual burdens bear;
And often for each other flows the sympathizing tear.

When we asunder part, it gives us inward pain;
But we shall still be joined in heart,
And hope to meet again.

—John Fawcett

CONCLUSION

Beloved, think it not strange concerning the fiery trial which is to try you, as though some strange thing happened unto you: But rejoice, inasmuch as ye are partakers of Christ's sufferings; that, when his glory shall be revealed, ye may be glad also with exceeding joy. —1 PETER 4:12–13

I BEGAN THIS BOOK IN THE COLD WINTER. Watching the falling snow through my window, I was longing for spring. Well guess what? The weather is changing. The sun is shining, temperatures have warmed up, and the grass is green. Little white and yellow dandelions are poking their pesky little heads up all over my lawn. The pillows are reinstated on the backyard swing—my favorite spot on the planet to spend time with God.

I walked into the backyard yesterday, and the Lord drew my attention to the trees along the back fence. Last year at this time we planted two peach trees and a plum tree. When I wrote the introduction of this book, those tender branches were frozen in winter's death grip. It seemed, to some degree, so was my life.

Today, those trees are in bloom. Beautiful pink blossoms unfold lazily in line with dozens of tiny, fuzzy peach buds. The sight held me hostage in the moment. The mystery and wonder captivated my heart. I wanted to shout to the neighborhood—"Hey everybody! I'm growing PEACHES!"

The trees are young—too young. I will need to pull the fruit off and let the branches grow stronger before we can enjoy the harvest in the coming years, but what a sight those peaches were! I stood there mesmerized, gently pulled branches aside, and leaned in close to get a better look.

When I did, it was as though God leaned in next to me and whispered, "Welcome to spring...."

OFF SCRIPT INDEFINITELY?

As of this writing, I'm a month away from the end of chemo. The doctor believes my cancer is gone. I have yet to meet with the radiologist to see where we go from here. Most certainly it will be autumn before my body begins to fully recover from the long months of treatments. The future holds plenty of questions and possibilities, but also lots of hope. From this vantage point, it appears as though my off script season may have an end in sight. As with all cancers, recurrence is a real possibility, so I continue to pray for God's will. If God leads me into recurrence at some future place, I know He will give the grace for the hardship when the time comes.

Like any normal person, I tend to hope that my trial will end and never return. But I'm sure there will be other trials. Didn't He tell us to expect these things?

> *Beloved, think it not strange concerning the fiery trial which is to try you, as though some strange thing happened unto you: But rejoice, inasmuch as ye are partakers of Christ's sufferings; that, when his glory shall be revealed, ye may be glad also with exceeding joy.*—1 PETER 4:12–13

I appreciate a predictable life. But I much more cherish the off script life. There's something special about being entirely removed from any personal agenda and completely and utterly encompassed by God's agenda. There's something special about a life direction that's completely out of your hands and totally in God's. That's the way life should be—all the time.

There's something special about greater weakness that He might receive greater glory.

This off script time has transformed my life dramatically. No matter what, I know that what I considered "normal" eight months ago will never quite return. But that's more than okay. Being off script with God is infinitely better than any script I could imagine on my own. This has been an amazing experience in the grace of God.

THE TEN DECISIONS

In these chapters we have explored ten passages of Scripture (with a few extras in between) and studied ten decisions that will transform your perspective in the midst of your trial. Here they are in summary:

1. *Love God, Trust God, Live for God*—Jeremiah 1
2. *Be of Good Cheer*—Matthew 14
3. *Be the Clay*—Jeremiah 18
4. *Cherish the Secret Places*—Isaiah 45
5. *Walk in the Spirit*—Galatians 5
6. *Wait for Him, Hope in Him*—Lamentations 3
7. *Try Your Ways*—Lamentations 3 and Hebrews 12
8. *Be Strong and Work*—Haggai 2
9. *Love Your Own*—John 13
10. *Strive Together for the Faith*—Philippians 1

SELAH — REST, RETUNE, REVIVE

Will you visit one more passage of Scripture with me before we close this book?

Psalm 3 was a passage that God took me to just before I was diagnosed with Hodgkin's. September of 2010, when

I had cancer and didn't know it, the Lord prompted me to study the psalms. That particular month I spent extra time in Psalms 1–25. But God showed me something really special in chapter 3.

Read it first:

> LORD, how are they increased that trouble me! many are they that rise up against me. Many there be which say of my soul, There is no help for him in God. Selah.
>
> But thou, O LORD, art a shield for me; my glory, and the lifter up of mine head. I cried unto the LORD with my voice, and he heard me out of his holy hill. Selah.
>
> I laid me down and slept; I awaked; for the LORD sustained me. I will not be afraid of ten thousands of people, that have set themselves against me round about. Arise, O LORD; save me, O my God: for thou hast smitten all mine enemies upon the cheek bone; thou hast broken the teeth of the ungodly. Salvation belongeth unto the LORD: thy blessing is upon thy people. Selah.—PSALM 3

The story behind this psalm is intricate. You can read its beginning in 2 Samuel 13. In that passage, King David's family is a mess after his sin with Bathsheba. His multiple wives have had multiple children who are now grown and sinning against one another. His son Absalom has killed his half brother Amnon in vengeance. Absalom ran as a fugitive. After three years, David is talked into allowing Absalom to return to Jerusalem, but he refuses to talk to him. Father and son go without speaking for two more years and their relationship only grows more bitter.

For many long and patient years after this point, Absalom quietly and subtly undermines his father's reign. He gradually wins the hearts of the people and finally decides it's time to kill his father and assume the throne of Israel.

Just in time, David learns of the plot, gathers his wives and loyal subjects and flees for his life. While hiding in the wilderness from Absalom, in a moment of great distress and dismay, David finds a quiet place with God and writes this Psalm.

It has three parts, each divided by an unfamiliar little word—*Selah*. It's a word we almost like to skip over when reading out loud. We don't know what it means, and we don't know how to say it. But it is significant—both to this psalm and to your life.

The word is a musical term with three probable applications. First, the word means "to rest"—referring to a pause in the music. Second, the word means "to retune or recalibrate"—referring to adjusting your instrument to the lead instrument during the rest. The third meaning is "to revive at a higher level"—referring to a key change in the music that takes the whole song up in strength.

In verses 1 and 2 David is dismayed and distraught by his trial. And then we see the word—Selah. Rest. Come to God and find total peace in Him. This is exactly what David did, and what we must do. Rest in Him. Be still and know that He is God.

In verses 3 and 4 David's attention is turned toward God and away from calamity. He re-tunes His heart to God's heart—to the lead instrument. And again we see the word—*Selah*. The principle is simply: take your eyes off of the trouble and place your eyes back on the Lord. Recalibrate your heart to Him and His truth.

Then verses 5–8 reveal a transformed man with a different perspective. David is revived—renewed in strength. His hope is restored and he is ready to face ten thousand enemies in God's power. He has re-engaged his struggle with new strength and faith. He is stronger than he was before because of His time with God.

When life goes off script—go to God, as David did. Rest in Him. Continually recalibrate your life to His truth. And then let Him revive your heart with greater strength. Rest, retune, and revive.

LORD OF MY LIFE

A friend of mine sings a song that, since I first heard it, has captured my heart. It's called *Seigneur De Ma Vie* (which is

French and means "Lord of My Life"). When I hear this song, I fight back tears and find myself wanting to physically get on my knees (wherever I am) in total surrender, worship, and submission to the Lord. Here are the words:

What can I give You after all is said and done?
How can the love that's in my heart be said or sung?
Just let me try to use my life to worship and adore You.

Lord of my life, Lord of my life.
Your touch is a gift from Love's own hand,
Destined for me since time began.
Safe by Your side, I'll walk in Your light.
I'll go where You go, hope of my soul,
Lord of my life.

You made the sun, the waves that dance upon the sea.
With every morning light You place Your faith in me.
The brilliance of Your gentle love will be my strength forever.
—Michael Puryear and Dwight Liles

I can't imagine living life without Him! He truly is the hope of my soul. I choose to follow Him wherever He goes. I accept His touch—even cancer—as a gift from Love's own hand, destined for me since time began. There is no place I'd rather be than safe by His side. He is and forever will be the Lord of my life.

Thank you for taking this journey with me. If you are not presently enduring a trial, I pray these chapters have helped you come to *expect* them and *understand* them through the lens of Scripture. I pray you are more prepared to travel through trouble without fear or discouragement, when the time comes.

If you are in the middle of a time of suffering or hardship, I pray you will personalize the ten decisions we've studied. I pray you will trust God in your testing. I pray His grace will be real to you.

And finally, I sincerely hope that in some special moment very soon, in the middle of your off script season, you will see the peach buds blossom, and the Holy Spirit of God will lean in close to your heart to gently whisper...

"Welcome to spring!"

ABOUT THE AUTHOR

CARY SCHMIDT serves as the Senior Pastor of Emmanuel Baptist Church in Newington, Connecticut. He and his wife, Dana, have been blessed with three children and have enjoyed twenty-three years of marriage and ministry together. Cary's passion is to love God, love his family, and point people to Jesus Christ—through teaching, preaching, and writing. He has written eleven books, including *Discover Your Destiny*, *Done*, and *Life Quest*.

Connect with Cary at CarySchmidt.com.

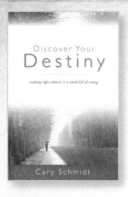

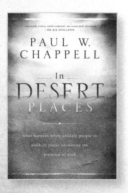

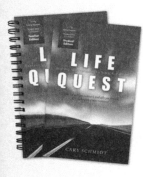

Visit us online

strivingtogether.com

wcbc.edu